Six Sigma
for Managers

Other titles in the Briefcase Books series include:

To learn more about titles in the Briefcase Books series go to
www.briefcasebooks.com
You'll find the tables of contents, downloadable sample chapters, information on the authors, discussion guides for using these books in training programs, and more.

A
Briefcase
Book

Six Sigma
for Managers

Greg Brue

McGraw-Hill

New York Chicago San Francisco Lisbon London
Madrid Mexico City Milan New Delhi San Juan
Seoul Singapore Sydney Toronto

McGraw-Hill

A Division of The **McGraw·Hill** *Companies*

0 AGM/AGM 0 9 8 7 6 5 4 3

ISBN 0-07-138755-2

Library of Congress Cataloging-in-Publication Data applied for.

This is a CWL Publishing Enterprises Book, *developed and produced for McGraw-Hill by CWL Publishing Enterprises, John A. Woods, President. For more information, contact CWL Publishing Enterprises, 3010 Irvington Way, Madison, WI 53713-3414, www.cwlpub.com. The editor was Robert Magnan. For McGraw-Hill, the sponsoring editor is Catherine Dassopoulos, and the publisher is Jeffrey Krames.*

Printed and bound by Quebecor World Martinsburg.

This publication is designed to provide accurate and authoritative information in regard to the subject matter covered. It is sold with the understanding that neither the author nor the publisher is engaged in rendering legal, accounting, or other professional service. If legal advice or other expert assistance is required, the services of a competent professional person should be sought.

> —*From a Declaration of Principles jointly adopted by a Committee of the American Bar Association and a Committee of Publishers*

McGraw-Hill books are available at special quantity discounts to use as premiums and sales promotions, or for use in corporate training programs. For more information, please write to the Director of Special Sales, McGraw-Hill, 2 Penn Plaza, New York, NY 10128. Or contact your local bookstore.

 This book is printed on recycled, acid-free paper containing a minimum of 50% recycled de-inked fiber.

Contents

Preface

Six Sigma is best described as a journey—a journey for business professionals who are truly committed to improving productivity and profitability. Six Sigma isn't theoretical; it's an active, hands-on practice that gets results. In short, you don't *contemplate* Six Sigma; you *do* it. And doing it has proven to be the fast track to vastly improving the bottom line.

The Six Sigma story began in the 1980s at Motorola, where it was first developed and proven. In 1983, reliability engineer Bill Smith concluded that if a product was defective and corrected during production, then other defects were probably being missed and later found by customers. In other words, process failure rates were much higher than indicated by final product tests. His point? If products were assembled completely free of defects, they probably wouldn't fail customers later.

This is where Six Sigma took off. Mikel Harry, Ph.D., the founder of the Motorola Six Sigma Research Institute, further refined the methodology, to not only eliminate process waste, but also turn it into growth currency—regardless of the specific type of service, product, or market sector. The rest, as they say, is history.

Six Sigma statistically measures and reflects true process capability, correlating to such characteristics as defects per unit and probabilities of success or failure. Its value is in transforming cultural outlooks from complacency to accomplishment across the spectrum of industry.

Most companies function at four sigma—tolerating 6,210 defects per one million opportunities. Operating at six sigma creates an almost defect-free environment, allowing only 3.4

defects per one million opportunities: products and services are nearly perfect (99.9997%). Eliminating defects eliminates dissatisfaction.

This all sounds good in theory, but how do you put it into practice? Well, Six Sigma is about arming your human "assets" with the training, resources, and knowledge to solve problems. It's also about taking a leadership journey to guide those assets toward ever-increasing achievement. Six Sigma asks hard questions about your processes and gets the data that supports them. It provides solutions that fit your unique processes.

And that's why I wrote this book—I want to share the Six Sigma story to show you how to achieve greater growth and improved customer service. Intense, results-driven, and ultimately exciting, Six Sigma eliminates wasteful variation, changes business cultures, and creates the infrastructure you need to initiate and sustain greater productivity, profitability, and customer satisfaction rates. In the following pages, you'll find out *what, why,* and *how* Six Sigma works, so you can start on your own Six Sigma journey.

Chapter Highlights

In Chapters 1 and 2, you'll learn the basics about Six Sigma and why you should put them into practice. I'll show how Six Sigma makes you more competitive at every level—from streamlining internal processes to improving your external market position. You'll also learn how to engage employees as you transform cost into growth.

Building on this base, Chapter 3 introduces the key role of business metrics in your Six Sigma initiative—demonstrating the value of hard data vs. opinion when analyzing the productivity of a given process. It will show you in factual terms just what your cost of poor quality is and how you can begin to correct it.

Chapter 4 gets into kicking off your Six Sigma initiative. It provides the essential guidelines, tips, and planning phases you need to get it right. By properly readying your organization, you can lay the best foundation for a successful implementation of

Six Sigma. And here's where the power of people comes in—
Six Sigma is predicated on educating and using your people to
direct and make phenomenal changes and sustain the benefits.

Everyone has a role to play in Six Sigma, from executives
to line workers, and Chapter 5 gives you an overview of who
does what to get Six Sigma under way. From champions to
black belts, green belts to project teams, you'll get a good
understanding of the scope and "mind share" of Six Sigma. This
is not a sidelined, occasional quality program. Six Sigma is an
all-out effort involving every single person in the organization in
a full-time, front-and-center focus on your operations.

Chapter 6 gets into the specific phases that Six Sigma uses
to dig deep into identifying the causes of waste or defects in
organizations. The four-phase approach known by its acronym,
MAIC—measure, analyze, improve, and control—is the heart of
any Six Sigma initiative. Within each step are specific actions
and directions that systematically point you toward identifying
the vital few variables that determine your quality outcomes.
Once you complete MAIC, you will have the necessary data and
answers that solve problems and return hidden dollars to your
bottom line.

Following up on all you've learned so far, Chapter 7 takes a
detailed look at all the necessary statistical tools and shows you
how to use them to pull all your data together. This is where "the
rubber meets the road" in Six Sigma. Statistics allow you to discover and isolate the vital few factors that are affecting your quality and performance. The tools presented in this chapter will help
you find and then fix the streams of variation in your processes.

Chapter 8 delves into how you should select projects to get
the most from MAIC. It examines "good" and "bad" projects,
what they mean to you, and how to tell the difference. Chapter 8
also introduces you to a statistical strategy that demonstrates the
optimal way to narrow down your search for projects, select the
most appropriate one, and begin investigating the money trail.

Chapter 9 then takes you into the world of sustaining Six
Sigma; it shows you how to keep the momentum going and

realize an ever-expanding return on investment. This is where knowledge transfer happens: as you and your teams transform theory into practice and become experts in the methodology, you will share the strategies that create an extraordinary "ripple" effect throughout the organization.

As you delve into Chapter 10, you will have the opportunity to review real case studies and final reports about Six Sigma projects. The object of this chapter is to further demonstrate that Six Sigma is not a passing fad, but rather a real-world business tool that returns positive financial results across the business spectrum. The evidence of its success is found in the proven results achieved by the companies profiled here.

Chapter 10 also introduces you to Design for Six Sigma, an extension of the basic methodology that shows you how to optimize your new design processes or products, to delight customers and return excellent financial results. From start to finish, this book is dedicated to one proposition—helping you explore and implement Six Sigma for better performance and profitability.

As a manager, you are uniquely positioned to unlock the extraordinary, untapped potential of your staff by introducing and initiating a Six Sigma program in your functional area. Employees are your greatest assets; Six Sigma knowledge and tools can give them almost limitless potential to transform your company—one project at a time.

Special Features

The idea behind the books in the Briefcase Books series is to give you practical information written in a friendly person-to-person style. The chapters are short, deal with tactical issues, and include lots of examples. They also feature numerous boxed sidebars designed to give you different types of specific information. Here's a description of these sidebars and how they're used in this book.

These boxes are designed to give you tips and tactics that will help you more effectively implement the methods described in this book.

Smart Managing

These boxes provide warnings for where things could go wrong when you're trying to prepare for and undertake a six sigma initiative.

These boxes highlight insider tips for taking advantage of the practices you'll learn about in this book.

Every subject has its special jargon and terms. These boxes provide definitions of these concepts.

It's always important to have examples of what others have done, either well or not so well. Find such stories in these boxes.

This identifies boxes where you'll find specific procedures you can follow to take advantage of the book's advice.

How can you make sure you won't make a mistake when implementing six sigma? You can't, but these boxes will give you practical advice on how to minimize the possibility.

Acknowledgments

Doing Six Sigma requires a team effort, and writing this book was no exception. First, I thank my wife Kelly for her unfailing encouragement and support throughout the course of this project and my ongoing Six Sigma journey. I am indebted to my colleagues and staff, especially to Peggy Dolowy and Elisabeth

Wisthoff, without whom this book would not have been possible. I also am grateful to John Woods of CWL Publishing Enterprises, who invited me to share my Six Sigma story and make its publication a reality. Bob Magnan, also of CWL, did excellent work in editing the manuscript that has become the book you now hold. Ultimately, my greatest appreciation must be extended to the innumerable champions and black belts who believe in and *live* the Six Sigma methodology. Their insights and leadership testify to the impressive power of knowledge in action, and I salute each and every one of them for their contribution and dedication.

About the Author

Since 1994, Greg Brue, CEO of Six Sigma Consultants, Inc. and Master Black Belt, has implemented Six Sigma methodologies for some of the world's most recognized companies.

Greg trains Corporate Champions and mentors CEOs, senior executives and company directors. A regular guest speaker at major business events and quality conferences, he also conducts Six Sigma seminars and monthly Executive Boot Camps. Greg supports numerous corporate Six Sigma implementations by maintaining direct contact with Black Belts, Master Black Belts, Champions, and senior managers.

Drawing on his considerable expertise, Greg developed the *Seven Principles of Problem-Solving Technology* to encapsulate and communicate the vision, purpose and results of Six Sigma. As a result, he has been instrumental in changing the mindset and infrastructure at major corporations—empowering organizations to achieve significant measurable results. Experienced and expert Six Sigma practitioners, Greg and his team provide the corporate community with the vision, velocity and quantum gains required to decrease defects and increase profitability.

For more information about Six Sigma Consultants, visit www.sixsigmaco.com.

What Is
Six Sigma?

Knowledge is power.
—Francis Bacon (1561-1626)

Do you know, do you really know, what's going on in your organization? The assertion that knowledge is power rings as true today as it did four centuries ago. In any industry, organization, or daily process, when you don't know *what* you don't know, it's going to cost you. For too many organizations the costs (often hidden) of defects and waste in the way they operate are huge.

Having processes in which errors occasionally occur may not seem such a big deal. But when you consider how many errors may be lurking in company-wide processes, the monetary impact on overall productivity, customer satisfaction, and profitability multiplies dramatically! The Six Sigma approach to managing is all about helping you identify what you don't know as well as emphasizing what you should know, and taking action to reduce the errors and rework that cost you time, money, opportunities, and customers. Six Sigma translates that knowledge into opportunities for business growth.

> **Key Term**
>
> **Process** Any repetitive action—be it in a transactional, manufacturing, or services environment. The Six Sigma methodology collects data on variations in outputs associated with each process, so that it can be improved and those variations reduced.

Many companies believe that dealing with errors is just part of the cost of doing business. But you don't have to accept that faulty logic. With Six Sigma, you can eliminate most errors, reduce your costs, and better satisfy your customers.

Six Sigma Defined and Explained

Six sigma is a statistical concept that measures a process in terms of defects. Achieving six sigma means your processes are delivering only 3.4 defects per million opportunities (DPMO)—in other words, they are working nearly perfectly. Sigma (the Greek letter σ) is a term in statistics that measures something called standard deviation. In its business use, it indicates defects in the outputs of a process, and helps us to understand how far the process deviates from perfection. (We'll get into the statistics in later chapters.)

> **Key Term**
>
> **Sigma** A term used in statistics to represent standard deviation, an indicator of the degree of variation in a set of measurements or a process.
>
> **Six sigma** A statistical concept that measures a process in terms of defects—at the six sigma level, there are only 3.4 defects per million opportunities. Six Sigma is also a philosophy of managing that focuses on eliminating defects through practices that emphasize understanding, measuring, and improving processes.

A sigma represents 691462.5 defects per million opportunities, which translates to a percentage of nondefective outputs of only 30.854%. That's obviously really poor performance. If we have processes functioning at a three sigma level, this means we're allowing 66807.2 errors per million opportunities, or delivering 93.319% nondefective outputs. That's much better, but we're still wasting money and disappointing our customers.

How well are your processes operating? Are they three sigma? Four sigma? Five?

Most organizations in the U.S. are operating at three to four sigma quality levels. That means they could be losing up to 25% of their total revenue due

> **Key Term**
>
> **Defect** A measurable characteristic of the process or its output that is not within the acceptable customer limits, i.e., not conforming to specifications. Six Sigma is about practices that help you eliminate defects and always deliver products and services that meet customer specifications. The sigma level of a process is calculated in terms of the number of *defects* in ratio to the number of *opportunities* for defects.

to processes that deliver too many defects—defects that take up time and effort to repair as well as creating unhappy customers. Is that good enough? The answer is simple. No it's not when you could be doing a lot better. Helping you do that is what this book is about.

The central idea of Six Sigma management is that if you can measure the defects in a process, you can systematically figure out ways to eliminate them, to approach a quality level of zero defects.

So, in short, Six Sigma is several things:

- A statistical basis of measurement: 3.4 defects per million opportunities
- A philosophy and a goal: as perfect as practically possible
- A methodology
- A symbol of quality

Six Sigma in Context

Let's take an example, an all-too-familiar scenario: lost luggage at the airport. Many of us have experienced the frustration of watching the baggage carousel slowly revolve while waiting for luggage that never arrives. The system is far from perfect. But just how far, in sigma measurement terms?

In general terms, the baggage handling capability of many airlines is performing at around the three sigma level. That means there are about 66,000 "defects" for every one million luggage transactions, which equates to an approximate 94% probability that you'll get your luggage. Is that good enough? Certainly not for the customers whose bags are among the "defects." The "defects" increase costs for the airlines, because employees must deal with misplaced luggage and unhappy passengers. And those "defects" can result in lost business in the future.

If the airline moves to six sigma in luggage handling, it clearly pays off in terms of lower costs and happy passengers, who are then more likely to fly with that airline again.

As Figure 1-1 indicates, operating at anything less than six sigma levels means your processes have higher probabilities of delivering defects.

It may seem like three sigma is good enough. After all, if

Sigma Level (Process Capability)	Defects per Million Opportunities
2	308,537
3	66,807
4	6,210
5	233
6	3.4

Figure 1-1. Probability of defects of different sigma levels

there are 66,807 defects out of a million, that means that 933,193 things went well—93.319% perfection.

But if the airline is taking comfort in those statistics, it's losing money and losing customers. Consider this three sigma level from another perspective.

For *customers*, three sigma represents highly unsatisfactory performance. The airline is not meeting their most basic expectation—that their luggage will be put on the same flight, to travel with them to the same destination. So the airline is likely to be losing many of those frustrated customers.

Three sigma is also costing money. Variations—time, waste, and errors—abound in the baggage-handling process: misrouting the baggage, reporting the problem, processing the report, searching, retrieving, and finally delivering the lost luggage. When you translate the 6% probability gap of missing luggage into monetary terms, the hard cost of this defect can be much higher than 6% of the overall cost of handling luggage—perhaps several million dollars per year. If the baggage-routing process were improved, the margin for error would be reduced and the allocation of resources, both human and monetary, could be much more profitably used.

How many customers can your business afford to lose? How much money can your company afford to lose because of mistakes? Why accept it as normal to be running processes at only three sigma or four sigma when, by changing the way you manage your processes, you could get a lot closer to six sigma and all the resulting benefits.

Variation Any quantifiable difference between a specified measurement or standard and the deviation from such measurement or standard in the output of a process. Variation in outputs can result from many causes in the functioning and management of processes. An important goal of process improvement is to reduce variation in outputs.

Six Sigma uncovers the layers of process variables—in data terms—that you must understand and control to eliminate defects and wasteful costs. It's a management approach that aims to achieve the apex of quality by measuring, analyzing, improving, and controlling processes to root out defects and boost bottom-line results.

A Little History of Quality

Many people associate Six Sigma with the quality movement. So, it seems logical at this point to start from that perspective. How does Six Sigma differ from the "quality" programs you may have already experienced? To answer that question, let's briefly recap the history of the quality movement.

No understanding of the quality movement would be complete without mentioning the visionary W. Edwards Deming, best known for helping the Japanese revitalize their industries after World War II. His approach was radically new and had significant impact on the evolution of quality and continuous improvement programs in organizations around the world.

It is fair to say that Deming's management approach, which came to be known as Total Quality Management or TQM (though Deming didn't like that term), has changed the way thousands of companies conduct their operations. By the mid-1980s, the extent to which corporate management was focusing on *quality* was significant:

Total Quality Management (TQM) A management approach that focuses on the organization as a system, with an emphasis on teams, processes, statistics, continuous improvement, and delivering products and services that meet and exceed customer expectations. Six Sigma is a disciplined extension of TQM.

businesses adopting TQM underwent a major paradigm shift, a transformation of "unlearning" everything previously believed about business to create better products and services. They began to understand that quality did not require higher costs but more efficient and reliable processes that delivered defect-free outputs and that they had to focus on process improvement and customer satisfaction. TQM is an excellent foundation from which to build toward the next level of quality management, represented by the Six Sigma approach.

But Six Sigma is far more than the latest "quality" trend. The proof? Companies that have implemented Six Sigma have achieved outstanding financial results and developed a disciplined, pragmatic plan for improved financial performance and growth.

Companies such as Motorola, Texas Instruments, IBM, AlliedSignal, and General Electric have successfully implemented Six Sigma and reduced costs literally by billions of dollars. More recently Ford, DuPont, Dow Chemical, Microsoft, and

Six Sigma at Motorola

Six Sigma was conceptualized as a quality goal in the mid-1980s at Motorola because technology was becoming so complex that traditional ideas about acceptable quality levels were inadequate. As the number of opportunities for defects increases, the percentage of perfection must rise. In 1989 Motorola announced a five-year goal—a defect rate of not more than 3.4 parts per million—six sigma. This initiative challenged ideas of quality in the U.S. and changed the concept of quality levels. It was quickly no longer sufficient to measure quality as percentages (defects per hundred opportunities). Now the bar was raised, to measure defects per million or even per billion.

American Express have started working on instituting the Six Sigma methodology. But it's about more than money. Jack Welch, the CEO who started Six Sigma at General Electric, called it "the most important initiative GE has ever undertaken," and said that Six Sigma is "part of the genetic code of our future leadership."

Essentials of the Six Sigma Methodology

The Six Sigma methodology uses statistical tools to identify the *vital few factors,* the factors that matter most for improving the quality of processes and generating bottom-line results. It consists of four or five phases:

- *Define* the projects, the goals, and the deliverables to customers (internal and external).
- *Measure* the current performance of the process.
- *Analyze* and determine the root cause(s) of the defects.
- *Improve* the process to eliminate defects.
- *Control* the performance of the process.

We'll outline these phases in Chapter 6.

We should note that Six Sigma methodology is not rigid. Approaches vary, sometimes significantly. One of the variations is in the phases: some approaches use all five of the phases listed above, while others do not include the Define phase. Six

> **Key Term**
>
> **Vital few factors** Factors that directly explain the cause-and-effect relationship of the process output being measured in relation to the inputs that drive the process. Typically, data shows that there are six or fewer factors for any process that most affect the quality of outputs in any process, even if there are hundreds of steps in which a defect could occur—the *vital few*. When you isolate these factors, you know what basic adjustments you need to make to most effectively and reliably improve the outputs of the process.

Sigma professionals recognize that this approach is a kind of roadmap for improvement, and it doesn't matter if it's called DMAIC, MAIC, PCOR (from the Air Academy—prioritize, characterize, optimize, and realize), GETS (from GE Transportation Systems—gather, evaluate, transform, and sustain). The point is that this is a set of tools aimed at helping managers and employees understand and improve critical processes.

Six Sigma is based on a few key concepts, which we'll cover in later chapters:

- Defect
- Variation
- Critical-to-quality
- Process capability
- Design for Six Sigma

Six Sigma focuses on defects and variations. It begins by identifying the critical-to-quality (CTQ) elements of a process— the attributes most important to the customer. It analyzes the capability of the process and aims at stabilizing it by reducing or eliminating variations.

Simply put, Six Sigma management is about tying quality improvement *directly* to financial results. The Six Sigma goal is to link internal processes and systems management to end-consumer requirements. Six Sigma is a scientific approach to management, driven entirely by data. The Six Sigma methodology eliminates the use of opinion—"I think," "I feel," or "I believe." Six Sigma drives the organization to a more scientific means of decision making by basing everything on measurable data.

Focus on Engaging People and Changing Processes

The first thing to know about Six Sigma is that it

> **Process capability** A statistical measure of inherent variation for a given event in a stable process. It's usually defined as the process width (normal variation) divided by six sigma and quantified using *capability index* (Cp). More generally, it's the ability of the process to achieve certain results, based on performance testing. Process capability answers the question, What can your process deliver?

doesn't rely on the latest program fads or "magic pills" to fix organizations. It relies on old-fashioned hard work coupled with factual data and a disciplined problem-solving approach. It affects every aspect and level of an organization—from line workers to middle managers to CEOs—to transform your *people* and your *processes.*

As the first step in that transformation, the Six Sigma mindset considers you and your people as *assets,* rather than as *costs* (liabilities). That's right—you are as much an asset as any

piece of capital equipment, and you represent an investment with extraordinary potential for return. Shifting the perspective on people from liabilities to assets (or investments) is fundamental to Six Sigma.

Once you're thinking in terms of "human assets," it's equally important to realize the underlying monetary value of rooting out wasted materials and steps

> **It's Not Just the People**
>
> Managers often tend to focus just on people in their organization. When something goes right or something goes wrong, they look for a person to congratulate or to blame. The fact is that work gets done through processes executed by people; both successes and problems are usually the result of what lots of people do, not just one person. If you don't pay careful attention to both people and processes, improvement will not happen.

Seeing Employees as Assets

An easy way to understand the concept of human assets is to calculate their individual return on investment (ROI). For example, if an employee costs the business $50,000 a year and his or her activity produces revenue of $100,000, the employee has covered the costs and raised an additional 100%—the profit or return. So, the annual ROI for that employee is 100%. By calculating employee ROI, you can focus on making the most of them as assets invested in your business.

in processes, as this is key to unlocking the hidden return on your investment in people. And that's also another aspect of the Six Sigma approach to managing.

By changing the way you look at processes, by understanding the vital few factors that cause waste, error, and rework, you can improve the ability of your processes to deliver higher quality to your customers and to lower costs. Once you know which vital few factors to focus on, you can make improvements that deliver dramatic results.

Sound simple? It is once you put your mind to it. By putting your people to work at solving process problems with proven statistical tools, you eliminate not only errors, but also inaccurate speculation about why processes don't work. Again, instead of opinion, you arm yourself and your people with quantifiable information—based on facts, not hunches and guesswork. When you know the facts, you are in a position to fix the problems permanently and gain long-term benefits. In other words, you've leveraged the power of knowledge to transform performance.

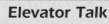

Elevator Talk

A CEO of a major corporation once asked me, "What's the 30-second elevator speech that explains Six Sigma?" My answer went like this: "Six Sigma is a problem-solving technology that uses your human assets, data, measurements, and statistics to identify the vital few factors to decrease waste and defects while increasing customer satisfaction, profit, and shareholder value."

Not Just Statistics, but Cultural Changes

Because it uses statistical terminology, Six Sigma is frequently perceived as a statistics and measurement program. This is not the case. The Six Sigma approach to management uses statistics solely as tools for interpreting and clarifying data. You focus on tool selection and the use and interpretation of data to drive decisions. Six Sigma practitioners also use computers and statistical software to take advantage of knowledge and speed the improvement process. The ultimate goal is to create Six Sigma companies—companies whose systems and processes are as perfect as possible, functioning at their best performance level.

To achieve that level of quality requires not just statistics, but changes in the culture of the organization. The Six Sigma approach is rigorous, requiring a deep commitment from the highest levels of management that permeates the entire organization. It requires a tolerance for endlessly questioning the validity of sacred company beliefs and the traditional ways "things are done around here." It also requires a sense of urgency—an understanding that, in order to solve the problems that undermine profitability and customer satisfaction, you need to involve your key people in actively implementing the Six Sigma methodology.

Culture Refers to the beliefs, expectations, ways of operating, and behaviors that characterize the interactions of people in any organization. It's about "how things are done around here" in an organization. Culture evolves over a long period of time and it often reflects the beliefs and behaviors of top management. Because Six Sigma affects the way things are done, its successful implementation will require a change in culture that may be profound.

Champions and Black Belts

The Six Sigma approach to management involves cultural change. Essential to this cultural change are key players known as *champions* and *black belts,* who act as agents to facilitate that change. These two titles play pivotal roles in the success of Six Sigma management, as we'll outline in Chapter 5.

A champion, generally selected from the ranks of upper management, serves as a coach, mentor, and leader—supporting project teams and allocating necessary resources.

Champion A senior-level manager who promotes the Six Sigma methodology throughout the company and especially in specific functional groups. The champion understands the discipline and tools of Six Sigma, selects projects, establishes measurable objectives, serves as coach and mentor, removes barriers, and dedicates resources in support of black belts. A champion "owns" the process—monitoring projects and measuring the savings realized.

A black belt leads a defined project on a full-time basis, working strictly on defining, measuring, analyzing, improving, and controlling processes to reach desired outcomes. Black belts do nothing else; their only responsibility is to root out variation and identify the vital few factors. They devote 100% of their energies to the chosen project, supported by project team members. So, why the martial arts terminology? Because a black belt's sole function is to focus on disciplined problem solving, practice specific skills, use a defined set of tools, and defeat the enemy—processes that deliver defective outputs.

There are other roles and levels in Six Sigma, which we'll cover in Chapter 5, but none as important as the black belt— the fully dedicated, thoroughly trained agent of improvement. The black belts are the people who apply the Six Sigma techniques to organizational problems and help change organization culture to focus on continuously get-

Black belt A full-time change agent trained in the methodology to solve product and process defects project by project with financially beneficial results. A black belt does Six Sigma analyses and works with others (often teams) to put improvements in place.

ting better in every aspect of performance. They harness the power of knowledge to achieve enhanced performance, customer satisfaction, and profitability—which is what it's all about. The average black belt improvement project results in a return of approximately $175,000 to the bottom line. And since black belts work on four to six projects per year, think what that can mean when multiplied by the number of potential projects in your organization!

Six Sigma is exciting. But it requires tenacity, mental toughness, and, above all, an unwavering dedication to the pursuit of perfection in every aspect of business operations. Once you've fully embraced that, the possibilities are virtually limitless in what you can achieve.

Six Sigma Applied

So how do you go about linking people to processes and practically applying what Six Sigma promises? That's the subject of this book. But, to give you a quick idea of what lies ahead, here's an example to show how Six Sigma works.

The CEO of a diversified *Fortune* 50 company gave the president of the financial services group the task of improving its net income by 10% and meeting a stretch target of 25%. The consequences of not meeting the CEO's directive would be dire—the division would be liquidated or sold off. A further wrinkle in meeting these requirements was that the CEO, a Six Sigma advocate, insisted this approach be used to achieve the stated breakthrough goal.

> **Breakthrough goal** A dramatic, near immediate, and significant improvement. In measurement terms, reaching a breakthrough goal represents an improvement of 60% to 80%.

Key Term

The president of the financial services group then gave her direct reports and management staff the task of improving net income by the stretch target of 25% and reiterated the CEO's directive to use Six Sigma methodology to do this. Clearly, all of the managers had

Meeting Stretch Targets

TOOLS A stretch target is the concept of looking beyond meeting basic requirements and exceeding your own expectations. When you understand that your defined goals are within reach, you need to shift your mindset to go farther, to reach higher, to stretch your capabilities. And when you do that, you realize far greater results than you initially thought possible.

What if you don't hit your target? You'll still have raised your bar: a stretch goal is a powerful way to motivate everyone to do better. Try it—you'll be surprised at how possible the "impossible" is!

their work cut out for them. They all realized that there was plenty of waste in their processes, but they didn't know how to identify the problems and eliminate this waste to reduce their costs.

Financial Services

Let's consider the financial services division, whose primary business focus is in loans. To find out which processes generated the most variation, the very first step was to ask the fundamental question: how do we make our money? Since the answer was "loans," managers needed to deploy the Six Sigma methodology to discover the facts about the dollars they were losing—what, who, when, where, and how in the loan process. In short, they needed to know what they didn't know.

As we mentioned earlier, Six Sigma begins by identifying the critical-to-quality (CTQ) elements of a process. In the residential loan department, the manager (we'll call him Greg) defined the CTQ metric as the loan approval process time. Specifically, he determined that the process should take only two days from receipt of the application. Anything else would be considered a "defect." The department was not meeting the specification, since the average loan approval took a full seven days. The five-day variance was the defect—the waste in the process.

Greg's loan processing department processed about 10,000 loans per month, with an average loan value of $25,000. The department was not measuring the money value of time lost in processing loans, which according to his specification meant losing five days of interest a month or 60 days a year. That translates to about two months' worth of interest payments on $25,000,000. Given an average interest-rate yield of 10%, this meant the department was losing approximately $400,000 per year because of the critical-to-quality factor of variance in loan processing time.

> **Critical-to-quality (CTQ)**
> Elements of a process that significantly affect the output of that process. Identifying these elements is vital to figuring out how to make the improvements that can dramatically reduce costs and enhance quality.

Once Greg identified the CTQ factor, he could specify the project—the way he would root out that waste by examining every process step and measuring the results. The goal was to identify what steps were causing this time variance.

There are three important components that characterize a Six Sigma project:

1. A critical-to-quality metric
2. An actual cost associated with a defect affecting the CTQ metric
3. A specific time frame for eliminating the defect to attain the CTQ metric

Now that Greg had his project parameters, he could assemble a team and lead them in his black belt role, focusing solely on determining the vital few factors standing between the process and its target performance.

His boss acted as the champion, ensuring that Greg and his team received all the necessary resources, removing any barriers, and informing upper management about the project's progress. Greg had a vested interest in the project's outcome: his division would benefit and so would he, since his performance bonus was tied to and measured by the project's results!

The Six Sigma five-phase sequence of DMAIC (Define, Measure, Analyze, Improve, and Control) was about to begin.

The Magic of DMAIC

Six Sigma statistical tools work like magic to uncover what you don't know. Yet you don't have to be a statistician to use them: you focus on selecting tools, using them, and analyzing data and let the specific software do the calculations. The five-phase process of DMAIC, described earlier in this chapter, uses a collection of tools and is a logic filter to lead you to the vital few factors affecting your process outcomes:

- *Define*—Determines the project goals and deliverables to customers (internal and external).
- *Measure*—Identifies one or more product or service characteristics, maps the process, evaluates measurement systems, and estimates baseline capability.
- *Analyze*—Evaluates and reduces the variables with graphical analysis and hypothesis testing and identifies the vital few factors for process improvement.
- *Improve*—Discovers variable relationships among the vital few, establishes operating tolerances, and validates measurements.
- *Control*—Determines the ability to control the vital few factors and implements process control systems.

In other words, the *Define* phase sets the targets for the Six Sigma project, the *Measure* and *Analyze* phases characterize the process, and the *Improve* and *Control* phases optimize the process and then maintain it.

In the Define phase, Greg determined that the project goal was to reduce the time for approving a loan to two days.

In the Measure phase, Greg started to map the loan application process. He identified four key areas: application form process, credit checking, management approval, and other areas, including rechecking and reapproving the loan application—virtually a built-in "rework" loop that was impacting the bottom line.

Once process mapping was complete, components were further broken down into the vital few inputs in the Analyze phase. In the case of the loan application form, the output was 100% completion of all form information. That created a baseline for defining a defect, as missing vital information on the form. Other process outputs causing waste were the four approval layers and unnecessary inspection points.

That may sound minor, but consider the rework and time value of "fixing" information at a later point in the process and then multiply that by the volume of loans. Once again, the exponential cost of a small defect soars.

In the Improve phase, the team developed the relationship equation between the application form (inputs) and loan funding (outputs) and prepared the way for the Control phase, which implemented changes. One of those changes was in the software. Now employees had to complete each field on the form before moving on to the next: the software would not let them skip ahead until they got the right information the first time.

Greg achieved his goals: by stopping rework on the application form, he reduced staff overtime, increased productivity, satisfied applicants with faster funding and met the breakthrough goal—reducing monthly operational costs by $60,000. Prior to the project, monthly loan processing costs were about $150,000; by removing $60,000 of waste, Greg trimmed that to $90,000 and achieved a 50% reduction in process time—yielding another $200,000 in additional interest payments. Now, that's a significant financial result! Needless to say, Greg got his bonus and the division stayed intact.

Turning Process Variation into Dollars

Process variation exists in every transaction, department, and business unit. From the micro to the macro perspective, using Six Sigma methods allows you to *define* goals and set specifications, *measure* process characteristics and estimate baseline capability, *analyze* the variables and identify the vital few factors, *improve* the process, and *control* the vital few factors and implement process control systems. Using the DMAIC approach, you can dig out waste and return hidden dollars to your bottom line.

Link Six Sigma Goals and Company Objectives

Six Sigma projects require well-defined problems and breakthrough goals. For example, in the case of the *Fortune* 50 company, the 10% net income goal is the immediate, defined goal. Not meeting it will result in clearly adverse consequences for the company. As long as you know what you're measuring and can tie that to the specific breakthrough goal, you've got the charter to achieve the outcome.

What Six Sigma Is Not

Six Sigma is not another quality program. That's an important point to emphasize.

Businesses exist for one purpose—to profitably serve customers. So it follows that any problem-solving initiative should do the same. Six Sigma uses your resources to fix identifiable, chronic problems. It proves its value by connecting outcomes to your bottom line.

Quality programs lay a valuable foundation in creating a quality mindset. But ask yourself if any you've experienced have generated specific financial results like Six Sigma. It's very possible you'll answer, "No," since a primary criterion for selecting Six Sigma projects is to return money to your balance sheet as the result of *full-time* efforts by dedicated resources.

Six Sigma is not theory. It's a practice of discovering the vital few processes that matter most. It defines, measures, analyzes, improves, and controls them to tie quality improvement directly to bottom-line results.

Six Sigma is an active, involved effort that puts practical tools to work to root defects at all levels of your organization. It's not a theoretical exercise: you don't *think* about Six Sigma—you *do* it.

Since the success of Six Sigma is directly linked to monetary outcomes, it generates real-world results. It uses the most readily available resources in an organization—its human assets. That means that positive, tangible results consistently show up wherever and whenever people are engaged in implementing Six Sigma techniques.

> **Six Sigma Is Not Another Quality Program** ⚠ CAUTION! ⚠
> Quality programs are valuable in that they can create a
> quality perspective and culture. But Six Sigma fixes iden-
> tifiable, chronic problems that directly impact your bottom line. Six
> Sigma projects are selected to reduce or eliminate waste, which trans-
> lates into real money.
>
> Six Sigma is not theory. It defines, measures, analyzes, improves, and
> controls the vital few processes that matter most, to tie quality
> improvement directly to bottom-line results.

Six Sigma is not a training program. Of course, practitioners
are trained in the methodology to ensure correct implementations and results. But Six Sigma is a business strategy that fosters a cultural shift at all levels. Permeating departments, functional groups, and all levels of management, Six Sigma changes
the outlook and practices of everyone in the organization.

From workers on assembly lines and bookkeepers in
accounting to operations managers and human resource personnel, training exists only to instill the method, facilitate transformation, and get financial results by attacking chronic defects
with proven statistical tools.

> **Six Sigma Myths**
> There are many myths and misunderstandings about Six
> Sigma. And as you participate in it, you'll probably hear at
> least one of the following:
>
> **Smart Managing**
>
> Six Sigma ...
> ... works only in manufacturing settings.
> ... doesn't include customer requirements.
> ... is repackaged TQM.
> ... uses difficult-to-understand statistics.
> ... is an accounting game without real savings.
> ... is just training.
> ... is a "magic pill" with little effort.
>
> Just remember that Six Sigma actively links people, processes, and
> outcomes in a rigorous, adaptable way to get you the results you're
> looking for. No matter the industry, business, product, or service, as
> you apply Six Sigma, you'll see the tangible results on your projects.

We began this chapter with an important quote—"Knowledge is power." Six Sigma helps you identify what you don't know, indicates what you should know, and helps you reduce defects that cost time, money, opportunities, and customers.

Will you achieve a six sigma level of quality, only 3.4 million defects per million opportunities—99.9997% perfect? That's really not the question. The question is "How much are process variations and defects costing you?" If you don't have that knowledge, you don't have the power to reduce or eliminate those problems and achieve significant savings.

This book will help you acquire that valuable knowledge about your processes—and about the Six Sigma techniques and tools to convert problems into profits.

Manager's Checklist for Chapter 1

❑ Six Sigma is the optimum level of quality for organizations, averaging 3.4 defects per million opportunities. It can be applied to any transaction in any business.

❑ Six Sigma is not a theoretical exercise, statistics, or training system. Although it's based on the foundation of TQM, Six Sigma is not a quality program.

❑ Six Sigma is the active deployment of statistical tools that eliminate variation, defects, and waste from all business processes and that are linked to significant financial results.

❑ Six Sigma deploys human assets and specified projects to effect lasting change in processes and meet stretch targets via a disciplined, five-phase approach that unearths variation and directs the precise steps for improvement.

Why Do Six Sigma?

The secret of success is constancy of purpose.
—Benjamin Disraeli (1804-1881)

Now that you are beginning to get a sense of the power of Six Sigma management, we explore in more depth reasons for adopting this approach.

How many reasons do you need?

Six Sigma allows you to achieve the constancy of purpose that is the secret to success, by focusing your efforts on understanding the variations in your processes and the defects that result. Here are the basic results:

- Money
- Customer satisfaction
- Quality
- Impact on employees
- Growth
- Competitive advantages

Money

Money is generally the most important reason for using Six Sigma. Processes that are inefficient waste time and other resources.

Senator Everett M. Dirksen, Minority Leader of the U.S. Senate from 1959 to 1969, is credited with the following remark: "A billion here, a billion there, and pretty soon you're talking real money." That comment about the fiscal foibles of government may make you laugh.

But how about this observation? "A dollar here, a dollar there, and pretty soon you're talking about thousands (and maybe even millions)." Sure, it's not as pithy as the apocryphal Dirksen quote—but it characterizes the situation in many companies, perhaps yours. And it's certainly not funny.

Here are a few questions to consider:

- What is the cost of scrap?
- What is the cost of rework?
- What is the cost of excessive cycle times and delays?
- What is the cost of business lost because customers are dissatisfied with your products or services?
- What is the cost of opportunities lost because you didn't have the time or the resources to take advantage of them?
- What is the total cost of poor quality (COPQ) in your organization?

Do you know the answers to these questions in terms of dollars? If so, then you know how important it is to reduce process variation and defects. If not, then you need to get the knowledge that gives you the power to make the necessary changes.

Key Term

Cycle time The time it takes to complete a process from beginning to end, consisting of work time and wait time. It is the case that, for many processes, wait time is longer than work time.

> **Cost of poor quality (COPQ)** Total labor, materials, and overhead costs attributed to imperfections in the processes that deliver products or services that don't meet specifications or expectations. These costs would include inspection, rework, duplicate work, scrapping rejects, replacements and refunds, complaints, loss of customers, and damage to reputation.
>
> These are costs that would disappear if there were no quality problems. An important goal of Six Sigma management is to reduce or even eliminate the COPQ—which for traditionally managed organizations has been estimated at between 20% and 40% of budget.

Customer Satisfaction

How important are your customers? In other words, where would you be without them? We all recognize this question as fundamentally important—but our answers reveal a wide range of perspectives.

I recall a comic strip that showed a professor looking out through his window at the campus and musing, "This would be a great job—if it weren't for all those students." You may laugh, but many managers and employees seem to feel that way about their customers.

Try this simple test. Walk around your company and ask people to complete the following sentence: "Our customers ...." You might be surprised at the perspectives expressed.

You must attract and satisfy and keep customers. Otherwise, you obviously won't stay in business long. But what role do your customers play, besides being a source of income?

The better you satisfy your customers (current and potential), the healthier your revenue. You know that. But do you know how to satisfy customers most effectively?

Six Sigma focuses on the critical-to-quality (CTQ) expectations of your customers: that's what matters most. By using Six Sigma management methods, your company can target the vital few factors in your processes that are allowing variations and defects that keep you from meeting the CTQ expectations of your customers. You can better align your business goals with the requirements and expectations of your customers.

How Do Your Customers Understand Quality?

The critical-to-quality (CTQ) concept in Six Sigma allows you to focus on improving quality *from the perspective of the customer*. Managers and employees all have some ideas about what constitutes quality for their products and services. That's good—but it doesn't put cash in the coffers. Find out which aspects of your products and services are vital to the customer and in what ways. Then you can set standards for delivering quality that matters to your customers.

Numerous case studies in various organizations have demonstrated the effects of Six Sigma management on performance in terms of customer satisfaction. In every process, product, or service, there's potential for better satisfying your customers. And that translates into money.

Focusing on the customer is an absolute business requirement. The pressure is overwhelming to perform, produce, and deliver faster, better, and cheaper. As technology has reshaped the speed of business and the quality movement has focused on the customer, customer expectations have changed. With access to the Internet and other channels of information and distribution, customers know more and have greater freedom to choose among products and services and companies. And they tend to choose and continue to patronize companies that deliver the highest quality at the lowest price in the least amount of time.

Six Sigma helps you get there by showing you how to find the "breakthrough points" in your processes. That means not only identifying the waste streams in your processes, but also understanding all the elements that create them.

You're familiar with the basic business term, *cost of goods sold* (COGS), and the comparable equivalent *cost of services sold* (COSS). This standard accounting term sums up all the expenses incurred to produce goods or services. It's a line item in any annual report. Six Sigma takes you inside that figure. It asks you the question, what is *in* the COGS or the COSS? With Six Sigma, what you find in the COGS or the COSS are opportunities to reduce costs. Then you can use Six Sigma tools to get rid of waste and reduce cycle times in ways that directly translate into improving CTQ factors for customer satisfaction.

In Chapter 1 we discussed a process stream (baggage delivery) that was defective (didn't deliver all items to the right place at the right time) and increased the COSS (incurred to report, locate, handle, and deliver missing items). If the process were perfect, the airline could save $8 million annually—which would go directly to its bottom line.

In addition, it would more effectively meet the expectations of its customers. Since it's important to customers to get their baggage quickly and conveniently, the airline would also increase its passenger miles and thus its profits.

Although it's simplistic to assert, "The customer is always right," it's good business to focus on meeting the expectations of customers—and no business at all, after a while, if you fail to do so. It's the premise of any business venture, but a goal that can get lost in the details. Six Sigma helps organizations focus on those details, to identify the vital few factors and make improvements that matter to the customers.

In the case of the airline described in Chapter 1, the customers expected the right luggage would be delivered to the right place at the right time. That very simple standard for satisfaction

Customer Satisfaction

"Customer satisfaction" is an overworked phrase. But when we break it down in a Six Sigma mindset, we refocus on its critical importance.

First, a "customer" is a person—not an organization—who buys something from you and with whom you have a relationship. Second, "satisfaction" is to be free of doubt, suspicion, or uncertainty about a product or a service. The word assumes that the product or service will fulfill the customers' needs and meet certain standards.

Those standards are defined by the *customer*—not the *organization*. If you don't understand what your customers want, you can waste time and resources making improvements that don't matter to the customers—and miss improvements that customers consider vital.

How Do You Like Your Coffee?

At a recent conference in a hotel, I asked participants what they expected in their coffee breaks. The answer: "lots of good, hot coffee!" When I asked the hotel banquet staff what they needed to provide, they agreed on good, hot coffee. But the two groups differed in their CTQ expectations.

Beyond coffee, the staff was concerned with providing linens, china, attractive displays, and extra snacks. However, the customers wanted a fast line for refills, high-capacity restrooms nearby, and access to telephones. Of course, customers don't want dirty cups or grubby linens, but they don't care much about ice sculptures.

So, here's the bottom line. The hotel is putting time and money into things that matter less to the customers and missing out on things that customers expect.

should be the basis for CTQ measurement for customers. Anything less than that is a defect.

When the airline fails to meet that most basic expectation, it dissatisfies its customers and is likely to lose some of them—and perhaps others who will hear complaints about lost baggage. We all know the phrase: "You never get a second chance to make a first impression." There's something to that—and a dollar value.

Value and Benchmarks

A key step in making improvements that matter to the customers is to determine which processes add value and which do not—from the customers' perspective. The concept of distin-

Value-added Any part of a process for which the customer is willing to pay. Value-added activities would be those involved in producing goods or delivering services.

Non-value-added Any part of a process for which the customer is not willing to pay. Non-value-added activities would include, for example, moving or storing raw products, approvals by various managers before something can happen. Such activities do little or nothing to satisfy customers. They only add costs, so they should be targets for elimination.

guishing between value-added activities and non-value-added activities is simple, but it can be difficult to work with that distinction, particularly when the processes have been in place for a while and/or the people involved are secretive, defensive, and/or territorial.

Once you've determined the value content of your processes and know which ones affect CTQ customer issues, you can then move on to understanding how your processes measure up. You do that through benchmarking, both internal and external. (We'll discuss benchmarking in Chapter 3.)

> **Benchmarking** A method for comparing a process, using standard or best practices as a basis, and then identifying ways to improve the process.

To briefly show how benchmarking works, let's return to the residential loan processing department in Chapter 1. Imagine that you're a customer waiting for the department to process your application. You're in a hurry. In other words, your CTQ requirement is promptness. But one week passes, then two, and then three ....

The lending institution, by not meeting your CTQ requirement, risks alienating you (and probably many other customers) and increases its cost of services sold (COSS). Of course, if it raises its fees to cover those costs, it's likely to lose even more customers.

Each functional group in the organization—customer service, sales and marketing, finance, information technology, accounting—plays a part

> **Choose Your Benchmarks Carefully**
> Don't benchmark only similar processes in the same industry, unless you want to quickly improve a very defective process. Also, be cautious about benchmarking your competitors: that makes sense only if you know that their processes are better.
>
> Think in terms not of the *process*, but of the *purpose* for the process. That way, you can identify dissimilar processes from which you can learn. For example, our airline in Chapter 1 could think beyond baggage, to study national package delivery services.

in delivering what the customer wants. Each group has processes that should work together to serve the customer. Are those processes the best they can be? Clearly not, since loans are delayed by nearly a month. So the residential loan department needs to benchmark its processes against processes in other divisions to discover waste, so it can then work to eliminate it.

Greg, the manager of the residential loan department, decides to start benchmarking internally. He determines which loan department is processing the most loans with the lowest defects. Then it's a question of studying how the processes in that department work better and finding ways to improve his department's processes.

Here are some basic guidelines for benchmarking your processes.

- Select a process for which to establish a benchmark.
- Estimate the costs of doing a benchmarking study.
- Select and train a team to do the study.
- Choose the key metrics to be studied.
- Develop tools to collect the data.
- Test the methods you plan to use to analyze the data.
- Analyze your process for the key metrics.
- Collect data on benchmark subjects.

We'll get into benchmarking in more detail in Chapter 3.

Plugging Up Profit

A spark plug manufacturer in the Midwest runs 14 manufacturing lines. We fixed one line and saved the company $35,000. How? By finding and fixing a simple, yet CTQ defect that was wasting money in its processes. That line's spark plugs did not meet customer expectations.

We took the process apart, reduced it to its basic elements, and found that the ceramic piece was not aligning with the metal part. We corrected this simple problem and eliminated the defect that was adding to the COGS of that part. The leveraging effect of this improvement throughout the plant was staggering—multiplying that $35,000 by the remaining 13 lines.

Greg could also examine how the loan process works in competing companies. Maybe one aspect is better with Alpha Savings and Loan, another with Big Money Loans, and yet another with Consumer Loans.

Whether you benchmark internally, externally, or both, it's essential to ask key questions about why your performance differs and to determine how you measure defects and yield rates.

Quality

Another reason for using Six Sigma is the value and impact of committing to quality as a goal in a very practical way. People who might not understand and appreciate other quality initiatives are more likely to recognize the value of Six Sigma, because the focus is essentially simple—to reduce or eliminate mistakes.

But what are the advantages of improving quality, other than to reduce costs and satisfy customers? Quality is an ideal of extreme power. Consider only the following advantages of focusing on quality:

- It inspires employees.
- It instills a culture and an attitude.
- It creates an image in the market and the community.
- It attracts investors.

And Six Sigma is not just quality, but a six sigma level of quality. That's close to perfect—99.9997%.

Why not just 99.379%—four sigma? That's the level of quality achieved by many major companies. Because that goal is not high enough. It's been calculated that, if 99% were good enough, we would be accepting the following:

- Every hour the postal service would lose 20,000 pieces of mail.
- Every day our drinking water would be unsafe for almost 15 minutes.
- Every week there would be 5,000 surgical operations that go wrong in some way.

- Every month we would be without electricity for almost seven hours.

From an Ideal to a Practical Goal

Quality guru Philip Crosby was one of the first practitioners to focus on preventing defects. While working at Martin-Marietta from 1957 to 1965, he created the concept of zero defects. At that time, organizations considered the ideal of zero defects unrealistic. About 20 years later, Six Sigma set a goal of 99.9997%—just .0003% short of zero defects.

Impact on Employees

There are also benefits of Six Sigma that don't translate into dollars—at least not directly. The effects on employees can be powerful.

Let's briefly consider a few of those effects.

Six Sigma inspires employees. When the company is committed to improving its processes, to meeting customer expectations, to cutting costs, employees will naturally feel motivated to do better. After all, how many of your employees actually want to do their jobs badly, to waste time and money, to fail to meet the expectations of your customers?

Six Sigma promotes morale and a sense of self-esteem. It gives employees the opportunity to make a difference. Every employee is important in Six Sigma. Some will be involved in special roles, of course, as black belts or green belts and so forth. But all of them will be encouraged to provide input on the processes around them. Every one of them has the opportunity to contribute significantly to Six Sigma efforts.

Six Sigma instills a culture and an attitude. It emphasizes the importance of viewing processes, products, and services from the perspective of the customers. Since all employees are customers when they're away from work, they can identify with customers—and particularly with their dissatisfaction and frustration when there are problems with products and services. They naturally empathize with customers, so they'll feel more positive about your company when it focuses on the customers.

Six Sigma promotes professional development for employees. The more employees know about Six Sigma techniques and tools and the more you encourage them to think critically about processes, the more competent they become. That competence not only helps your company, but also makes employees more valuable on the job market—which is an increasingly important consideration.

Six Sigma concentrates on systematic improvement of processes. That approach will appeal to the logic of your employees, many of whom have probably wondered why certain processes work in ways that seem illogical. How many employees have you heard complain about inefficient processes? Through Six Sigma, you're providing them with opportunities to improve those systems that confuse and frustrate them.

Those are some basic benefits of Six Sigma for your employees. And they definitely have an impact on your bottom line.

Growth

As you identify and correct process variations, you save on expenses—which means money to invest in growing your business. As you meet the requirements and expectations of your customers more effectively and achieve higher customer satisfaction, you increase your income—which means money to invest in growing your business.

The key to transforming costs into growth is in identifying the waste streams in your cost of goods or services sold (COGS or COSS) and making corrections in the processes.

> **Map Your Processes**   TRICKS OF THE TRADE
>
> In Chapter 1, Greg, the manager of the residential loan department, mapped out every step in the loan granting process, to find the bottlenecks and rework loops that added to the cycle time for processing loans. By digging into the COSS, he identified factors that were adding costs and then shortened the cycle time to meet the CTQ expectations of customers.
>
> Six Sigma begins with mapping processes, to understand every aspect of every targeted process. We'll cover this step in Chapter 7.

Competitive Advantages

Six Sigma allows you to become more competitive—regionally, nationally, or globally. At this point, you probably don't need any justification for that statement. A company that reduces its costs of doing business, meets the expectations of its customers more effectively and efficiently, earns a reputation for quality, and fosters a culture of dedication and pride will certainly enjoy advantages over its competitors. It can provide higher-quality outputs at a lower cost.

If you need further proof of the competitive advantages of Six Sigma, just check out the gains achieved by the companies that have invested in implementing Six Sigma:

- At General Electric, Six Sigma added more than $2 billion to the bottom line in 1999 alone.
- Motorola saved more than $15 billion in the first 10 years of its Six Sigma efforts.
- AlliedSignal reports saving $1.5 billion through Six Sigma.

Nobody can promise that you'll cut costs by billions, because performance results through Six Sigma are unique for each company. But it's been estimated that you should expect a return on investment of three or four times the costs of implementing Six Sigma. That should give your company a significant competitive advantage.

Are You and Your Company Ready?

This question may not seem to fit in a chapter titled "Why Do Six Sigma?" However, it actually fits in a negative way. If we ask the inverse of that question, Why *not* do Six Sigma?, the answer would be "If you and your company are not ready." That's because Six Sigma requires a solid and active commitment.

The top leaders of your company must be committed to the Six Sigma process. This means that they must fully embrace what you're doing. They must realize that the Six Sigma approach to management and process improvement is not a quick fix and that implementing this approach will require many changes in the conventional ways of operating. There are two levels of commitment required by your company leaders:

- They must commit company resources to help the Six Sigma initiative succeed.
- They must commit their time and energy to actively promote the initiative.

"Commitment" is a simple, often overworked term that has lost some of its punch in recent years. How are we using it here?

You're probably familiar with that classic illustration of the difference between *involvement* and *commitment*. When you're making eggs and bacon, the hen is involved—but the pig is committed.

The hen is busy laying one egg after another; what happens to those eggs doesn't affect the hen very much. The pig, on the other hand, is totally committed to the process! It's going to sacrifice its life to make the bacon.

Now, this analogy may be somewhat silly, but it makes the point about involvement and commitment. You and the other managers in your company need to be more like the pig and less like the chicken. It's not enough to just be involved in Six Sigma; you must be committed to making it work.

You've got to give it your all. Company leaders and other managers must be engaged; they need to function as champions and provide the support—financial and otherwise—to make the effort succeed. When you start Six Sigma, it's no longer business as usual—for anyone on the organizational chart. Now let's consider if your company is ready to do Six Sigma.

How Do You Rate?

To determine whether your company is ready for Six Sigma, you need to ask certain key questions. By asking them at the beginning of the Six Sigma process, you can gauge how you're doing now, and later, how far you've gone.

Does your company have a clear strategic course?

- Are the people in your company ready and willing to react to changes?
- How effectively does your company focus on meeting customer expectations?
- Are you ready to begin measuring the defect levels and yields for each service, product, and process?
- Are you ready to begin reducing defect rates by at least 50% over time?
- Are you ready to begin looking at how much you spend in fixing mistakes—the cost of poor quality?
- Are you ready to reduce the cost of poor quality by 25% over time?
- Are you ready to reduce your process cycle times by 50% over time?

By asking such key questions, you can gauge if your company is ready to determine the impact of defects and reduce the cost of poor quality and cycle time. Getting answers takes time, research, and careful analysis. It's not easy, it's not quick, but the results are worth the effort and time.

The Correlation Between Quality and Cost

Many managers hesitate to promote quality initiatives because they believe that the higher the quality of the outputs, the more they have to cost to produce. This is simply not true.

Of course, there are costs:

- **Direct payroll costs:** People will be devoting some or all of their time to Six Sigma.
- **Consulting costs:** You will likely be working with a consultant and a master black belt from that firm.
- **Training costs:** The key players in your Six Sigma initiative will need training, some extensive.
- **Improvement costs:** You'll be making changes, some perhaps quite expensive.

The prospect of those costs might make some decision makers hesitate. However, as many in the quality field have pointed out, intelligent, well-directed efforts to improve quality actually reduce costs. And, in fact, there can be a direct correlation between high quality and lower costs, if your approach is in that order. What I mean is that when you focus on improving processes rather than on reducing costs, costs come down naturally as you reduce process waste and inefficiencies. However, if you simply cut costs without considering the effect on your outputs, you'll likely reduce quality.

Manager's Checklist for Chapter 2

❏ In every process, product, or service, hidden defects are costing your company. Six Sigma will help you find and eliminate them so you can reach the critical-to-quality (CTQ) standards customers expect.

❏ Six Sigma requires that you truly understand customer viewpoints. You must really know what customers want, not go by what you *think* they want. You must ask what's important to them. What are their CTQ criteria?

❏ Study every aspect of your processes to understand the true cost of goods or services sold. By separating value-added activities from non-value-added activities, you can isolate the hidden waste streams.

❏ Benchmark your processes against internal and external peer groups and determine why your performance differs.

❏ Six Sigma success depends on you, your team, and the unqualified support of executive leaders. They must be committed to making it work. They need to lead, understand, and support the initiative throughout the organization.

❏ Six Sigma focuses on the direct relationship between quality and cost. Focus on improving processes to reduce waste and inefficiencies and costs will decrease naturally.

Setting Business Metrics

*When you can measure what you are speaking about,
and express it in numbers, you know something about it;
but when you cannot measure it, when you cannot
express it in numbers, your knowledge is of a meagre and
unsatisfactory kind. It may be the beginning of knowledge, but you have scarcely, in your thoughts, advanced
to the stage of science.*

—William Thomson, Lord Kelvin
(1824-1907)

In short, if you don't have measurements, you can't make
progress because you don't know where you are. Quite simply, everyone needs a scorecard. In business, the most important scorecard is profit. And if you're implementing Six Sigma
management, other important measures include the cost of
poor quality, the cost of goods or services sold, customer satisfaction, net income, and—yes—defects.

These are the factors that create "money situations": they
either add to or subtract from a company's overall profitability.

Business metric A unit of measurement that provides a way to objectively quantify a process. Any measurement that helps management understand its operations might be a business metric: number of products completed per hour, percent of defects from a process, hours required to deliver a certain number of outputs or provide a service, and so on. Business metrics provide data that Six Sigma managers can use to better understand their processes and identify target areas for improvement.

This is why you need to implement *metrics*—to quantify the effects of these factors. If you can measure your processes, you can understand them. If you can understand them, you can correct, control, and improve them and thus reduce costs while improving the quality of your outputs.

Most businesses have some version of measurement. After all, managers and executives need to calculate profits and losses, the cost of goods or services sold, and return on investment. But beyond the basics, how exactly do managers go about making decisions and changes that reduce costs, improve profitability, and foster growth?

Today, many organizations *operate by axiom*—that is, they accept and communicate certain statements they believe to be true about their operations. However, when managers are pressed to objectively justify their belief in these axioms and to explain why they provide appropriate guidance, they're often at a loss.

Committed to Quality?

We often hear business leaders say, "We are committed to quality." That's a standard axiom. But what does it mean exactly? How can you verify that? How do you quantify that?

You measure the extent to which goods and services are meeting customer expectations. After all, that's the basic criterion for quality. You measure every aspect of the goods, services, and processes that affect quality. By doing this, you remove opinions and emotions from the equation and replace them with facts and figures that verify or refute that claim of commitment to quality.

MISTAKE PROOFING

Get Data

Traditional management often operates by the "seat of the pants"—by tradition, by impression, by reaction to events, by gut instincts. The essence of Six Sigma management is to use objective data to make decisions.

A Little Statistics

Before we get into a discussion of how to set business metrics, we should return to a concept basic to Six Sigma—sigma. In Chapter 1 we defined it as "A term used in statistics to represent standard deviation, an indicator of the degree of variation in a set of measurements or a process." So, now we should elaborate a little on standard deviation and variation.

Variation

As defined in Chapter 1, variation is "any quantifiable difference between individual measurements." Any process improvement should reduce variation, so that we can more consistently meet customer expectations. But in order to reduce it, we must be able to measure it. So, how do we measure variation?

There are several ways, each with advantages and disadvantages. Let's take an example to show how these methods work.

Your company produces widgets. There are two lines that assemble the components, A and B. You want to reduce the variation in assembly times, so that the workers who package the components can work most efficiently—not waiting for finished widgets, not falling behind, and not being forced to work so quickly that they make mistakes.

The first step is to track assembly times. You gather the following data:

Process A: 3.7, 6.5, 3.2, 3.2, 5.7, 7.4, 5.7, 7.7, 4.2, 2.9
Process B: 4.7, 5.3, 4.7, 5.4, 4.7, 4.4, 4.7, 5.8, 4.2, 5.7

Now, what do those figures mean? We can compare the two processes in several ways, using common statistical concepts. (In reality, you would be collecting much more data than our 10 sample values, but we'll keep this example simple.)

If we use the *mean*, we find that line A averages 5.02 minutes and line B averages 4.96 minutes. That's very close. But we don't know which process varies more.

We can calculate the *median* value (the midpoint in our range of data). For A it's 4.95 and for B it's 4.7. That's close.

> **Mean** Average (more specifically called the *arithmetic mean*), the sum of a series of values divided by the number of values.
>
> **Median** Midpoint in a series of values.
>
> **Mode** Value that occurs most often in a series of values.
>
> **Range** Difference between the highest value and the lowest value in a series, the spread between the maximum and the minimum.

We can also calculate the *mode* (the value that occurs most often): for A, it would be either 3.2 (two times) or 5.7 (two times) and for B it's 4.7 (four times). The mode doesn't help us much here.

Based on these three measurements, what do we know about the variations in our two widget assembly lines? How do they compare? Which statistical concept best represents the variation in each line?

We don't know much about our variation at this point. Fortunately, there are two more concepts that we can use: *range* and *standard deviation*.

Range is easy to calculate: it's simply the spread, the difference between the highest value and the lowest value. The range for A is 4.8 (7.7 – 2.9) and the range for B is 1.6 (5.8 – 4.2). Now, that's a considerable discrepancy between A and B! The variation in process A is much greater than in process B.

But range is a rough measure, because it uses only maximum and minimum values. It seems to work OK in this case. But what if we had the following values?

Process C: 3.2, 6.5, 3.4, 6.4, 6.5, 3.3, 3.7, 6.4, 6.5, 3.5

The range for this set of values is 3.3, which suggests that there's less variation in process C than in process A, with a range of 4.8. But common sense tells us that the values in process C vary more, even if less widely.

We need another concept, something more accurate than range for calculating and representing process variation. That concept is standard deviation.

Standard Deviation

Standard deviation measures variation of values from the mean, using the following formula:

$$\sigma = \sqrt{\frac{\Sigma (x - \bar{x})^2}{n}}$$

where Σ = sum of, X = observed values, X bar (X with a line over the top) = arithmetic mean, and n = number of observations.

That formula may seem complicated, but it's actually simple to understand if we break it down into steps:

1. Find the average of the process values.
2. Subtract the average from each value.
3. Square the difference for each value (which eliminates any negative numbers from the equation).
4. Add all of these squared deviation values.
5. Divide the sum of squared deviations by the total number of values.
6. Take the square root of the result of that division.

So, when we do the calculations for process A and process B (fortunately, there are software applications that can crunch these numbers for us!), we get the following results:

A: standard deviation = 1.81
B: standard deviation = 0.55

These figures quantify what we observed, that the variation in process A is greater than the variation in process B. Our simple example uses only 10 values for each process, so

> **Key Term**
>
> **Standard deviation** Average difference between any value in a series of values and the mean of all the values in that series. This statistic is a measure of the variation in a distribution of values.

calculating standard deviation doesn't help us much more than simple observation. But when our measurements give us many more values, the concepts are more useful—and we appreciate even more the software that does all of these calculations for us.

If we plot enough values on a control chart (we'll discuss this type of chart in Chapter 7), we'll likely find that the distribution of values forms some variant of a bell-shaped curve. This curve can assume various shapes. However, in a *normal* curve, statisticians have determined that about 68.2% of the values will be within 1 standard deviation of the mean, about 95.5% will be within 2 standard deviations, and 99.7% will be within 3 standard deviations.

Your goal is to reduce the variation in your widget assembly processes. So you first need to determine how much variation is acceptable to your customer. Then, you use those values to set your *lower specification limit* (LSL) and your *upper specification limit* (USL). These are the upper and lower boundaries within which the system must operate.

In our example, we might determine that the customer (the widget packaging group) would be happy if the assembly lines took between 4 and 6

> **Specification limit** One of two values (lower and upper) that indicate the boundaries of acceptable or tolerated values for a process.

minutes (within 1 minute either way of the ideal time of 5 minutes). That would set an LSL of 4.0 and an USL of 6.0 around a mean of 5.02 minutes for line A and a mean of 4.96 for line B.

Since the standard deviation for A is 1.81, we're quite far from our goal, because the standard deviation is greater than the interval between the LSL and the mean (1.02) and the interval between the USL and the mean (.98) specification limits.

On the other hand, since the standard deviation for B is 0.55, we're already meeting our goal, because the standard deviation is greater than the interval between the LSL and the mean (.96) and the interval between the USL and the mean (1.04) specification limits. (Of course, we already knew that line

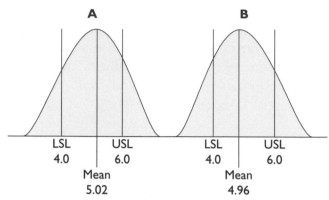

Figure 3-1. Bell curves showing results from two sets of measurements

B was meeting the customer's expectations, because none of the 10 times recorded in our measurement is above 6 minutes or below 4 minutes.)

Process Capability

So, how does all of this discussion of variation and standard deviation and curves relate to Six Sigma? The goal of Six Sigma is to reduce the standard deviation of your process variation to the point that six standard

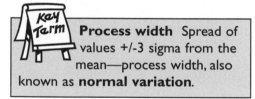

Process width Spread of values +/-3 sigma from the mean—process width, also known as **normal variation**.

deviations (six sigma) can fit within your specification limits.

You may recall the concept of process capability from Chapter 1, defined as "a statistical measure of inherent variation for a given event in a stable process." The *capability index* (Cp) of a process is usually expressed as *process width* (the difference between USL and LSL) divided by six times the standard deviation (six sigma) of the process:

$$Cp = USL - LSL/6\sigma$$

The higher your Cp, the less variation in your process. In our case of the widget assembly lines, with an acceptable allowance of +/–1 minute from the ideal mean difference, reaching a six sigma level of quality would mean reducing the standard deviation of both process A and process B to about .166. The Cp of process A is 1.105 and the Cp of process B is 3.636.

There's a second process capability index, Cpk. In essence, this splits the process capability of Cp into two values.

Cpk = the lesser of these two calculations:
USL – mean/3σ or mean – LSL/3σ

In addition to the lower and upper specification limits, there's another pair of limits that should be plotted for any process—the *lower control limit* (LCL) and the *upper control limit* (LCL). These values mark the minimum and maximum inherent limits of the process, based on data collected from the process. If the control limits are within the specification limits or align with them, then the process is considered to be *capable* of meeting the specifications. If either or both of the control limits are outside the specification limits, then the process is considered *incapable* of meeting the specifications.

> **Control limit** One of two values (lower and upper) that indicate the inherent limits of a process.

"Sadistics"

A friend who was studying statistics had a young daughter who referred to the subject as "sadistics." From the mouths of babes....

At this point, you may not be able to perform all of these calculations and others used in Six Sigma. That's why there's statistical software. You may not understand all the ins and outs of these concepts. That's why training is essential to any Six Sigma initiative.

What's important here is that you understand the basic concepts of Six Sigma measurements and better appreciate the importance of establishing metrics to track variation so you can improve processes. With that quick overview of the essentials, we can leave our imaginary example of widgets and return to the very real situation of your business.

Criteria for Business Metrics

So what are the criteria for establishing business metrics? The answer is surprisingly simple. The criteria relate to why you're in business and why you want to implement Six Sigma—to improve customer satisfaction and reduce costs. With that in mind, you need to establish metrics to help you achieve these goals.

Measurement is crucial to the success of your Six Sigma initiative. Your business metrics show you the ways to achieve dramatic improvements in your processes. They apply statistical tools to any process to evaluate and quantify its performance. They continually ask what outcome, or dependent variable, is a function of another, independent variable, to dig out the information that improves your performance.

It's a fundamental principle of the Six Sigma philosophy that you cannot improve quality unless you can measure it. This applies to any aspect of Six Sigma. If you're going to invest in measuring customer satisfaction, then you need to have a quality measurement system to track performance. In other words, your business metrics constitute your scorecard, the way you figure out where you are. To use another term, they form your dashboard.

The Dashboard Concept

The business dashboard as a metaphor for critical metrics to measure business performance originated years ago at General Electric. Just as you use the speedometer, oil gauge, battery indicator, fuel gauge, and other instruments to monitor the status of your vehicle as you drive, so you want to keep track of key indicators of the performance of your company. Like the dashboard gauges, your metrics allow you to continually assess your progress and detect any potential problems.

Your choice of business metrics and the importance you give them show what you value. If you value customer service, for example, you make it central to your business metrics. You put it on your scorecard. You include it in your dashboard.

Conversely, if you don't measure quality and don't follow up on any measurements, you give the impression that you don't care about customers or profitability. That impression affects the behavior and productivity of everyone in the department, division, or organization.

By instituting key business metrics across functions and groups and at every level, you directly link individual performance to measurable outcomes. This sends a clear message that not only do you care about customers and revenue, but so should everyone else, since they are accountable for the results measured by their particular metrics.

Question Everything

When you create metrics, you need to ask questions—new questions—and search for new results. If you keep asking the same questions, you'll keep generating the same measurements. That brings to mind that adage: "The height of insanity is doing things the same way and hoping for a different result." How many companies exemplify that insanity in managing their processes?

There's another quote to keep in mind:

Genius, in truth, means little more than the faculty of perceiving in an unhabitual way.
         —William James (1842-1910)

Six Sigma allows and even requires you to be a genius. The key to "perceiving in an unhabitual way" is asking questions ... and then questioning the answers.

When you begin setting up new business metrics and asking questions, you should begin with the fundamentals:

- Why do we measure this?
- Why do we measure it in this way?
- What does this measurement mean?
- Why is this measurement important?

Ask questions. Challenge answers. Put assumptions to the test. Confront conventions. At this stage you should tap people who are known for their critical thinking skills, whether they're familiar with the processes or not. Encourage them to question

---

CAUTION!

Measure Twice, Cut Once

A smart carpenter knows the value of making sure with the ruler before using the saw. A less careful carpenter spends a lot of money and time buying wood.

So why would you simply guess at ways to improve products, satisfy customers, and increase revenue? That's exactly what you're doing when you don't use metrics.

Sure, you might find a way to reduce expenses in a given process without using metrics. But how will the change affect customer satisfaction? Are there ways to improve the process as well as cut costs? Is the process even necessary?

Measure first and measure often. It's the best way to improve processes, meet customer expectations, and reduce costs.

---

and to challenge. That approach might be unusual in your company, but to do otherwise would be the height of insanity.

Whether you manage a small administrative staff or a large manufacturing division, by asking questions, examining the fundamentals, and establishing appropriate metrics, you're taking the right first step toward Six Sigma success.

Moving from Criteria to Metrics

How do you actually select appropriate metrics? You need to measure what's important, what's critical to your business. You know that key criteria are customer satisfaction and revenue.

So, let's start with customer satisfaction. For every product or service, you need to determine the expectations of your customers, particularly the critical-to-quality (CTQ) factors. What aspects of the product or service are key to your customers? For each aspect, what are your customers' expectations?

If you're producing widgets, for example, you might consider the following aspects: size, weight, durability, price, ease of use, versatility, colors, styles, availability, maintenance, service, warranty, and so on. For each of these aspects, you would determine expectations. How many sizes of widgets do they expect? Which sizes do they expect? How long do they expect a widget to last? What price do they expect to pay? How easy to use do they expect a widget to be? How long do they expect it to take to repair a widget? Do they expect a loaner widget?

For every product or service, there could be dozens or even hundreds of aspects. Focus on the aspects that are most important to your customers. For every key aspect, there could be several or many expectations. Once you determine the essential expectations, figure out ways to measure how well your product or service is meeting those expectations. Then, work backward through the process, to establish metrics for activities that are critical to meeting those expectations.

Make sure that all measurements are linked to bottom-line results. For example, if you're working on making your super widget more durable, you should focus on metrics for raw materials and assembly, but not on metrics for painting or packaging. For every metric, ask the question, how does this metric link to the bottom line?

With Six Sigma, this is a continual question—because Six Sigma is based on tangible financial results. Measurements must result in an identifiable impact on the bottom line.

Identifying CTQ factors is generally a laborious process. In one company, the Six Sigma team analyzed 800-1,000 processes, each of which had 100-120 different specifications. It identified the most critical factors that would lead to greater customer

> **Process mapping** *Key Term*
> Creating flowcharts of the steps in a process—operations, decision points, delays, movements, handoffs, rework loops, and controls or inspections. A process map is an illustrated description of how a process works.

satisfaction, lower costs, and/or greater ease of assembly. The team then mapped and prioritized CTQ factors to be targeted in Six Sigma projects.

Process maps allow a team to visualize the flow of products or the sequencing of activities. In so doing, it can locate steps that don't add value to the process. Eliminating such steps is an easy way to reduce cycle time and cut costs.

Smart Managing

Less Is More

When setting metrics, keep the numbers of measurements small. As you get into the Six Sigma mindset, it's natural to want to measure everything. Don't. The key here is quality over quantity. Select only a true set of indicators that will give you the needed information on process factors that affect customer satisfaction and revenue. When establishing a metric, you need to know why you're measuring it, why it's important, and what's causing the results.

Think back to the dashboard analogy. Driving would be more difficult if the dashboard contained too many indicators. The same is true with too many metrics. Select and limit measurements carefully. The essential indicators will provide the information you need.

It takes a lot of time and effort to identify CTQ factors, but without mapping each and every CTQ process, you won't get the information necessary to target areas for improvement and to fix problems.

Your metrics should provide data that enables you to solve performance problems in your processes as quickly as practical. They should also, consequently, be sufficiently sensitive to reveal changes of any significance. For a simple example, let's take our widgets. If the cycle time for the process of molding components averages three hours and seven minutes, a metric that tracks minutes might be sensitive enough. If the cycle time for the process of assembling those components averages 11 minutes and 54 seconds, then we'd want a metric that tracks seconds. If the cycle time for the process of packaging widgets averages four seconds, then our metric should be sensitive to tenths of a second at least.

CAUTION! **Avoid Bad Metrics**

When developing metrics, beware of the following:
- Metrics for which you cannot collect accurate or complete data.
- Metrics that are complex and difficult to explain to others.
- Metrics that complicate operations and create excessive overhead.
- Metrics that cause employees to act not in the best interests of the business, just to "make their numbers."

Metrics need to "slice and dice" in increments that capture small but significant changes and track them in terms of cost, time, and quality. They indicate the ability of a process to achieve certain results—your *capability index*, as defined in Chapter 1 and explained earlier in this chapter.

Be Sensitive

Set metrics to reveal changes of an appropriate magnitude, so you can monitor any significant variations in the process. What's significant? That depends on your baselines and your goals. It's important that your metrics capture change with a high enough resolution to enable you to take action to improve the process.

One of the innovations of Six Sigma is to establish metrics in terms of opportunities for defects. You'll recall from Chapter 1 that sigma levels are based on the number of defects

Kicking Field Goals

We can use metrics to study the performance of the field goal specialist on a football team. He must kick the ball between the goal posts—his *specification limits*. Any result outside those limits is a *defect*. We establish a *baseline*, by having him attempt a field goal 100 times. The number of successful kicks out of those 100 attempts is his *capability*.

Although the scoreboard registers only successes, that's not enough for us, because we want to improve his kicking process. So we want to measure his accuracy in terms of the exact center of the goal posts. The less his kicks deviate from that ideal, the more confidence we can have in our kicker.

So, we track the *distribution* of the kicks through the uprights. That allows us to calculate the *capability index* (Cp)—the distance between the goal posts divided by six times the standard deviation of his 100 kicks. (If the kicker tends to pull to one side or the other, we might measure this specific shift in the process with another capability index, Cpk.)

Now we not only know the percentage of correct outcomes, but also understand how we need to work on his kicking process to make it more reliable, less susceptible to circumstances that might cause variation, such as wind or wet turf.

per million opportunities (DPMO). By calculating quality levels according to the complexity of the product, service, or process, Six Sigma allows for metrics that make it easier and more realistic to compare performance for products, services, or processes that differ.

Here's a simple example. William and Mary both work for Acme Wax Fruit Company. William runs the apple production line, which melts wax cubes, pours the wax into molds, and then dips the resulting item into a wax bath of another color. Mary manages the shipping department for the citrus fruit division: she's responsible for the employees who handle the inventory (oranges, lemons, and limes) in the warehouse, the employees who load the trucks, and the truckers who deliver the goods. The processes that William and Mary manage vary greatly, but since some of the metrics established for them are in terms of DPMO, it's possible to know that they are currently at 81,900 DPMO and 74,700 DPMO, respectively, and set a goal for next year of three sigma—66,800.

And that's how, with metrics using DPMO, you can compare apples and oranges!

Making Metrics Work

Measuring for measurement's sake isn't going to tell you what you need to know. By always asking about the function of each metric and linking it to your key criteria, you'll know where you are and where you need to go. Here are the types of questions you need to ask as you establish metrics:

• What are our business metrics?
• What are the measurement criteria?
• Do the metrics link to the criteria?
• Do they correlate to competitive advantage?
• If they don't correlate, what must we change?

These questions may be obvious, but they help keep you and your staff on target for Six Sigma results. As long as you can answer these questions, then you're setting your business metrics right. Remember: if you don't ask the right questions, you won't get the right answers.

Leadership by Example

Establishing metrics requires dedication, focus, and logic. It also requires leadership. As manager, you must serve as a model of critical thinking and courage to challenge the status quo and underlying assumptions. You must ask yourself and people in your division and even throughout the company why all of you do the things you do. When you challenge, when you ask new questions and start measuring the answers, you demonstrate leadership that gets positive financial results from digging into the hidden streams of waste. You need to know exactly what a particular process is actually providing, its cost of goods or services sold, and its capability.

The criteria for business metrics are found everywhere in an organization—in services, products, and processes. By asking new questions, you can develop metrics that will help you better understand your processes by eliminating opinions and percep-

Discovering COPQ

To discover the COPQ, you may need a structured approach:

- *Internal failure*—costs resulting from defects found before the customer receives the product or service (examples: scrap, rework, reinspection, retesting, downgrading, downtime, reduced productivity, failure analysis).
- *External failure*—costs resulting from defects found after the customer receives the product or service (examples: warranty charges, complaint adjustments, returned material, allowances, replacements, compensation, damage to reputation).
- *Appraisal*—costs of determining the degree of conformance to quality requirements (examples: inspection, testing, process control, quality audits).
- *Prevention*—costs of minimizing failure and appraisal costs (examples: quality planning, policies and procedures, new design reviews, in-process inspections and testing, supplier evaluations, education and training, preventive maintenance).
- *Non-value-added activities*—costs of any steps or processes that don't add value from the customers' perspective.

CAUTION!

Don't Neglect the Human Costs

The cost of poor quality usually has a personal side. People who work in an organization that has problems with quality may be affected in various ways: poor morale, conflicts, decreased productivity, increased absenteeism, health problems related to stress, burnout, and higher turnover. These human consequences add to the cost of poor quality.

tions and dealing with numbers. Those metrics are your dashboard, the indicators of your status and your progress.

What Is the Cost of Poor Quality?

As you develop and use your metrics, undoubtedly you'll come across a critical, key indicator that lurks in services, products, or processes, regardless of business focus—the cost of poor quality (COPQ). The cost of poor quality rears its ugly head virtually everywhere. It's a financial iceberg: you see only the tip of it, but its full impact is huge.

Measurement reveals the sources of COPQ so you can take the steps necessary to eliminate them. As you target and resolve the root causes of poor quality, you boost quality, which in turn will have positive repercussions throughout the service and delivery cycle.

Financial Linkage of Metrics and Results

There are two main concepts governing metrics. The first is *knowledge*. Your metrics provide knowledge about your processes and help you develop better metrics. The second concept is *alignment*. Your metrics must align with your strategic goals for performance.

When implementing business metrics, it's critical to link them to your overall performance. This is the key. If your metrics don't align with your performance, then they can't possibly tell you anything you really need to know.

Here's an example. A direct-order clothing company sets forth its basic performance goals in a series of "principles of doing business." These principles establish the following points:

- The company does everything possible to make its products better and never reduces the quality of any product to make it cheaper.
- The company accepts any return for any reason at any time. It guarantees its products unconditionally: there's no fine print and no arguments.
- The company ships all orders quickly: items in stock ship the day after the order is received; customized orders take a day or two longer.
- The company trains its sales and service employees to know its products, to be friendly and helpful, to spend the time necessary to take care of customers.
- The company has lower prices because it operates efficiently.

These principles frame, in straightforward terms, the company's performance goals. The metrics should align with these goals. Since product quality is important, the company might assess conformance of raw materials with specifications, but not focus on cycle time. Because products are guaranteed unconditionally, the company might not calculate the value of returns, but should concentrate instead on reasons for those returns. The company promises next-day shipping; it would necessarily track turnaround time, to ensure keeping its promise but not to try to reduce that time. The company encourages employees to take care of the customers; if it measured contact time, that metric would not be in alignment with the performance goal of complete customer care. Since the company keeps its prices low through efficiency, it would have a series of metrics to measure factors throughout its operations, but probably not in areas that affect quality or attention to customers.

This quick example shows how your metrics should link to your performance goals. Otherwise, you won't be getting the knowledge about your processes that you need to improve them—or you'll be working on making improvements that won't matter to your customers or could even disappoint, frustrate, or

It's a simple point, but worth repeating: if your
t align with your performance, then they can't pos-
anything you really need to know.

Guidelines for Metrics

Here are some steps to help you select, set up, measure, and
get results from your metrics. These guidelines will help you
realize the financial connection of your metrics effort. They are
simple, internal things you can do to get the metrics in place
and get the information you need.

Step 1. Get leaders involved. Since they set company strategy,
they need to be involved in how the metrics are linked to
achieving it. I cannot stress enough how important it is for executive leadership to actively support you. Your Six Sigma initiative will require a company-wide commitment of human and
other resources. When upper managers are engaged, you've got
the freedom to make real changes—based on what the metrics
tell you and the entire organization.

Step 2. Visually represent your metrics. Prominently display
them in charts, graphs, and diagrams, to show your employees
what you're trying to do and how they are involved in delivering
information and correcting the processes.

Step 3. Metrics must respond quickly. Your measurement systems must provide feedback promptly, so you can identify problems and correct them as soon as possible. They should not be
cumbersome or take a long time to yield data.

Step 4. Metrics must be simple. They must clearly communicate the CTQ information you need. Avoid setting up complex
measurements that are difficult to use. You want direct information to take direct action.

Step 5. Metrics should drive only important activities. Make
sure they relate to regular activities and processes. You need to
assess the most important factors to measure—both in terms of
COPQ and COGS/COSS—and then make sure that what you

examine will result in information that's relevant. Your goal is to get at waste and defects and correct the processes to reduce costs. Your metrics must reflect that, no matter what.

Step 6. Limit the number of metrics. Generally, you should implement no more than 10 metrics at a given time. Why? You want fast feedback. Metrics exist for this purpose only. If you get bogged down in measurements, you can lose time and focus, employees will get confused, and upper managers may lose track of what you're doing. Don't get flooded with metrics that clog the entire activity stream. 10 or fewer—that's the rule!

Step 7. Take corrective action. Once you have feedback, you and your team should take corrective action as soon as possible. You want to maintain the momentum of your Six Sigma initiative and have it pay off as soon as possible. Act quickly, then move on to your next project and set new metrics.

Problems with Metrics

It's easy to get caught up in measuring things, so that you focus so much on quantifying defects that you forget about also quantifying the effects. Here's an example. If you're setting metrics for your secretaries, you might include a measurement of typos in terms of 1000 characters (opportunities). So you determine that George averages 5 typos, Sarah averages 7, and Pat averages 8. Well, obviously George is the most accurate, right? Yes—if you quantify defects only. But what about the effects on your customers? George generally has more problems with names, while Sarah and Pat check names carefully. Since customers are usually more bothered by mistakes with their names than mistakes with other words, George would suffer by comparison with Sarah and Pat. That's one of the problems with being too focused on counting defects alone.

Along these lines, we should caution against focusing on averages. The usual way to represent a series of figures is by finding the average. But consider the potential complication. Here's an example. Your goal is on-time deliveries. For your three delivery drivers this month, you calculate averages of 15.3 minutes late, 24.7 minutes late, and 6.3 minutes late. So, you conclude, Driver 3 has the best average. That's true, but the averages don't show everything. They don't show that Driver 3 is often as late as Drivers 1 and 2, but occasionally arrives 20 to 30 minutes early. That helps compensate for being late—but it inconveniences the customer when dock workers have to cut their lunch short to unload the truck. The averages also don't show that Driver 1 has several times been late by 45 minutes, while Driver 2 has been late by 20 minutes at most. Six Sigma allows you to measure variation in a process, to calculate standard deviations from the mean, so you have a more accurate picture of the process.

A final point to make here is that metrics should use units that everybody understands. If, for example, we want to establish metrics for incomplete shipments, what constitutes "incomplete"? Does it matter how many items are missing? Do you account for the relative importance of the items to the customer? If so, how? The problem of an incomplete shipment is worse if the customer refuses delivery, but how do you measure that effect? How do you establish a metric that doesn't require any of the employees to make judgments when they track the data?

How do you establish appropriate, accurate metrics? You tap the experience of the employees who are closest to the processes. You hold meetings to discuss your attempts at establishing metrics and you encourage everyone to find fault with them. Then, finally, as you use your metrics, encourage one and all to report any questions or problems with them.

Baselines

After you've determined the metrics that will provide you with the most important information about your processes, you use them to establish baselines. A baseline indicates the current status of your performance.

In a way, baselining is similar to the thorough physical examination that you would undergo before beginning an exercise regimen. Just as your doctor would check out basic indica-

tors of health, your baseline activity should measure key input variables,
key process variables, and
key output variables.

> **Baseline** A standard for comparisons, a reference for measuring progress in improving a process, usually to differentiate between a current state and a future state.

The focus of Six Sigma
lies in a simple three-part
formula: $Y = f(X)$. It represents the basic truth of a process:
Output (Y) is a function of Input (X). This is just a mathematical
way to state that variables or changes in inputs and the process
will determine outputs.

The activity not only provides baselines, of course, but it
also serves as a good test of your metrics. As you apply your
metrics to establish baselines, you may find problems with
some of them: maybe you need to modify metrics, drop metrics, and/or add metrics. Sometimes metrics that make sense
on the drawing board just don't work as well when we put them
to use.

Benchmarking

When you've established your baselines, you understand the
current state of your processes, you know where you are. The
next step, benchmarking, allows you to figure out where you
want to go with your processes. After all, as that great philoso-
pher, Hall of Fame baseball player, and quotable coach, Yogi
Berra, once observed, "If you don't know where you are going,
you will wind up somewhere else."

As we mentioned in Chapter 2, benchmarking is a method
for comparing a process, using standard or best practices as a
basis. Through benchmarking, you can establish priorities and
targets for improving the process and identify ways to do so.

At this point, you know what processes you want to benchmark and you've got your metrics. Now what?

The next step is generally to identify benchmarks for your target processes. The benchmarks may be internal or external.
Since most Six Sigma initiatives use benchmarks outside the
company and since that's a more complicated practice, external

benchmarking will be our focus here. (If you decide to use bench-marks within your company, it's considerably less difficult.)

How do you identify benchmarks? First, you consider your competitors. Which among them has target processes that per-form better than yours? You may know that through competitive intelligence or through media reports. Also, as you probably realize, the Web has become a great source of information on companies. Articles that would have gone unnoticed in small, local publications or data that would have been buried in a report are now out there for you to access.

Next, you collect data on the target processes. How you do this depends on the processes, the benchmarks identified, and the sources of information. Use your creativity and investigative instincts and skills. You may be able to get information from public domain sources, through the library or the Web. Some companies provide information in white papers, technical jour-nals, conference presentations, panel discussions, and so forth, or in materials for vendors and customers or advertisements. You may need to develop questions for a survey to be conduct-ed by mail, by telephone, by fax, or by e-mail. You may decide

---

⚠ CAUTION!

Keep It Legal and Ethical

Benchmarking can be risky business. To minimize the likelihood of misunderstandings, ethical slips, and legal problems, you should follow the simple Code of Conduct scripted by the International Benchmarking Clearinghouse, a service of the American Productivity & Quality Center (www.apqc.org/free/con-duct.cfm). It provides guidance through outlining the following eight principles:
- Legality
- Exchange
- Confidentiality
- Use
- Contact
- Preparation
- Completion
- Understanding and Action

to take the most direct approach, to contact companies and arrange site visits. You could also enter into a benchmarking partnership, in which each partner would gain information about the others in exchange for sharing information on its own processes. Another possibility is to work with a competitive intelligence firm.

Once you've completed your benchmarking studies, you should have data for each of your key metrics for the targeted processes. Then, you're ready for the next step.

Gap Analysis

You've used your key metrics to establish baselines for your target processes. You've gathered benchmark data to show how your processes could be performing. Now, you compare. In technical terms, you do a gap analysis, to quantify the gaps between where you are now and where you want to be.

> **Key Term**
>
> **Gap analysis** A technique used to compare a current state and a target future state.

Your gap analysis enables you to set goals for improving your processes and to develop strategies for improvement. You may not be able to set goals for improving every aspect of every process; you may need to prioritize. You may not be able to set ideal goals; especially early in Six Sigma implementation, you may want to set goals that allow you to achieve important gains quickly, to prove the value of Six Sigma. Then you can set your sights on breakthrough goals.

Putting It All Together

This chapter has been long, but there are a lot of variables involved in setting business metrics. Here's an example to show how they might all come together.

In a recent study, I found that a particular company's SG&A (Selling, General, and Administrative expenses) was 500% higher than that of the nearest competitor in its peer group. Why? What was the difference?

We determined that the company was overstaffed—way overstaffed! By first benchmarking its performance and figuring out its baseline, we had the knowledge to select the metrics necessary to realign the company. The first thing the company had to do was to set a new short-term direction to get to a minimally acceptable level of performance. That was the goal for creating a new company baseline, which in turn set in motion the actions that translated the goal into a real and better baseline.

At that point, the company was ready to ask more searching questions or, in other words, to set up metrics. It could ask questions about why competitors performed better with less and how they sustained their performance. At the same time, it could examine its own processes and functions to yield the crucial answers—or data—that improve profitability.

Here's a summation of the basic steps in setting metrics:

- **Start with your customers.** What expectations are important, critical to quality?
- **Establish key, consistent metrics.** What metrics belong on your dashboard?
- **Determine baselines.** What is the current state of your processes?
- **Benchmark processes.** Who's doing the same or similar things better than you?
- **Set goals.** Easier goals can give you quick successes; more ambitious goals can help sustain your Six Sigma initiative.

Keeping Your Process Capability

Let's conclude this chapter by returning to the question of process capability. What capability does your target process demonstrate in terms of your metrics? What are the factors affecting that capability? How do you keep and control it?

Once you know that, you can maintain the optimum and consistent performance of the process. It doesn't matter whether you're delivering goods or services, once you know what you can achieve, you can retain it for sustained productivity and profitability.

Consider the loan department example from the first two chapters. Greg (the manager) and his staff needed to achieve and keep the best average performance in a given month to maintain customer satisfaction. In his case, this meant ensuring that the loan application process flowed freely, unrestricted by unnecessary steps or inspections. Once he and his team figured out their barriers and removed them, they could achieve their best average performance and maintain it.

Six Sigma is not a one-shot exercise; the extraordinary commitment of resources throughout your organization must be validated continuously. Six Sigma is dedicated to making permanent changes to realign your processes through the implementation of metrics. It enables you to know what you can expect from your people and processes. By maintaining and controlling that performance, you keep the value and purpose of your Six Sigma efforts in the forefront of all your activities, both today and into the future. Consider it a return on investment with far-reaching effects.

Manager's Checklist for Chapter 3

❑ Measurement is crucial to the success of your Six Sigma initiative. Your business metrics are your scorecard that makes a lasting difference between business as usual and dramatic improvement in productivity and profitability.

❑ Metrics apply statistical tools to evaluate and quantify the performance of any process.

❑ Metrics show you the true cost of poor quality and indicate the direct relationship between quality and cost: when you increase the former, you can reduce the latter—resulting in even greater customer satisfaction.

❑ Metrics must be clear and simple and must yield information quickly, so you can improve your processes continuously.

Implementing Six Sigma

*The difference between failure and success is doing a thing **nearly** right and doing it **exactly** right.*
—Edward Simmons (1852-1931)

So now that you know the basics of Six Sigma, the reasons for using Six Sigma, and the essentials for the business metrics that are the core of Six Sigma initiatives, it's time to practice what I've been preaching. It's time to implement Six Sigma and turn theory into profit.

Before you get started, pay attention to the following key do's and don'ts—quick, simple reminders of how you can best proceed to get the most from your Six Sigma initiative.

From metrics to project selection, as long as you follow the basic principles expressed in the following two lists, you can ensure that your efforts are working at maximum capacity for lasting results.

Getting Started: The Do's

Do **keep the focus on results.** Have a clear vision of where you are and where you want to be in terms of decreasing costs and increasing bottom-line profits. Use a project tracking system to monitor results. You can usually get one from a qualified implementation partner (a consultant brought in to teach the Six Sigma methodology). After asking the hard questions like "What caused this?" and "What is this a function of?" you need to find out the answers. Again, keep it under control—you want to work on the vital few factors, not the trivial many.

Do **embrace customers.** Remember those critical-to-quality expectations of your customers. Achieving phenomenal business growth depends on how well you understand and meet those expectations. So stay in touch with customers and keep current on what they want from you in terms of price, quality, and delivery. Remember: it's not about what *you think* they want, but what *they say* they want.

Do **plan for success.** Proper planning ensures you will meet your goals. Planning gives you the milestones and progress reports that indicate how well and fast you're reaching your goals.

Do **communicate the commitment company-wide.** Tell everyone what you're doing and what you intend to accomplish. From the CEO to the production line, every employee should have a vested interest and role in your Six Sigma projects—a sense of ownership goes a long way toward driving true commitment and enthusiasm at every level.

Do **demonstrate the commitment of company leaders.** Make sure your company leaders actively show their own commitment to your Six Sigma success. They need to be visible and show all employees that they're prepared to do whatever it takes to get the results you want. They do this by serving as mentors and champions, freeing up company resources and breaking down barriers to support your projects.

Do **empower your key human resources.** Pick the right people to lead your Six Sigma project teams—and empower those key players. Within the Six Sigma phases of Define, Measure, Analyze, Improve, and Control, make sure that your black belts and team members have the essential quality tools for a particular project.

Do **provide on-site mentoring for black belts.** As part of that empowerment, you must assure your black belts of your total support for their projects. Their access to information or data, from within your company and from outside, and their interpretation of it must be unrestricted. By applying Six Sigma statistical tools in tandem with critical data, black belts can mine hidden dollars. As long as you and other champions and your implementation partner are available on-site to mentor them, black belts will provide the return on investment you want.

> **Key Term**
>
> **Implementation partner** An outside expert engaged in introducing, training, and supporting your Six Sigma initiative.

Do **choose an implementation partner who will actively assist in screening and selecting Six Sigma projects.** A qualified outside expert who is engaged in introducing, training, and supporting your Six Sigma initiative is of vital value in helping you select not only the right project, but also the right people to run it.

Do **be patient at the inception of your Six Sigma initiative.** Six Sigma projects require the front-end commitment of training, time, and resources to deliver the end results. You and your employees have to learn how to select projects, develop metrics, and assign key roles, and that takes time. Proper planning makes for profitable outcomes—you can't rush results.

Do **claim and advertise early "wins."** Although you need to be patient as your projects get under way, it's also very important to communicate and celebrate each milestone of success. This keeps your team's enthusiasm high and demonstrates how Six Sigma is working. Tell employees, upper management, customers, and vendors; they need to know the value of your efforts every step of the way.

Do **benchmark.** Benchmarking is a key step. By formulating a benchmark plan that looks at both internal and external performance standards, you can conduct the right gap analysis to know where you are and where you should be.

Do **establish project baselines and goals.** You need to know your current defect levels, your defect-reduction targets, and how much money you want to save. Then you'll have the right baselines and goals to measure the progress of your projects.

Do **get advance buy-in from your controller.** It's important— especially when you're talking about company money—to be "in sync" with the company controller! You need to be operating from the same monetary baseline: you both need to agree on how you calculate real savings and how you distinguish between hard dollar and soft dollars. If you work together, your results can be verified by the controller, which further validates all your Six Sigma work.

> **Hard dollars** Savings that are *tangible*—exact, quantifiable cost savings, such as reduced hours, reduced inventory levels, etc.
>
> **Soft dollars** Savings that are *intangible*—expenses that you avoid, such as not increasing hours, inventory, or physical workspace.

Getting Started: The Don'ts

Don't **make Six Sigma a massive "training" exercise.** Six Sigma focuses on real, tangible financial results. You and your staff need to learn how to implement it and get started. You don't need to send your employees to seminar after seminar to further develop their Six Sigma skills. Of course, they need to know what they're doing, but once they're trained as black belts, they'll know exactly how and what they need to do to get at the money in waste and defects. That's why you invest the time and money in training them. I'm not saying that people shouldn't keep their skills current and sharp, just that they have to use what they've learned and put the theory into practice. This is all about getting results in bottom-line profitability.

Don't **take a "Big Bang" approach to Six Sigma.** In other words, don't train all employees at once to be Six Sigma practitioners. Surgical strikes with the right people and the right projects are far more effective. Most organizations can't manage a lot of changes simultaneously or support hordes of black belts or projects. So keep it focused, train selected people to get projects under way, and capture clear gains case by case. As you achieve results, other company divisions can embrace the methodology.

Don't **focus resources on reworking training material.** A big part of implementing Six Sigma is necessarily training. But, although you certainly want to train your people well, particularly your black belts, you don't want to spend excessive time "tweaking" training materials to fit your exact business model. You should certainly relate training materials to your business focus, but recognize the overall and adaptable nature of Six Sigma and get busy applying it, not discussing it.

⚠CAUTION!⚠
Don't Tweak the Training

An excessive focus on reworking training information can really hamper a Six Sigma initiative. I recently realized just how much when I partnered with a major manufacturer of aircraft and other transportation equipment to implement Six Sigma.

The company was prepared to launch Six Sigma, the entire staff was ready to get started, and the momentum was strong. Then came the training material. Anxious to be sure that the material tied in with their industry and business, company leaders and managers focused almost exclusively on adjusting the material. Their rationale was that they had to tweak it to understand it better. This sounds logical, but *nine months* later, they were no further ahead in implementing Six Sigma and realizing the gains. Just think of what they could have accomplished!

Continually reworking your training materials can be as costly as reworking your processes. Keep the focus on getting results.

Show Me the Money!

Smart Managing

Sometimes controllers can be Six Sigma barriers, as they fear their budgets will be cut if they report the money saved by your projects. For instance, in some companies, if a project saves $10 million in a $100 million budget, the savings will be eliminated, forcing controllers to operate with a $90 million budget. You and your executive champion need to signal that the purpose of your Six Sigma projects is to *save* "hidden" money, not to *eliminate* it. Although you want to drive that hidden revenue to the bottom line, you will also use it in other areas. This way, Six Sigma projects work to *reduce costs*, not to *slash budgets*. When they understand, controllers will probably want projects to succeed as much as you do.

Don't let the controller waffle about your savings calculations. Controllers play an important role and must be included in your Six Sigma initiative at the outset. They need to know that your executive leadership expects them to cooperate and support your efforts. Controllers who refuse to acknowledge soft vs. hard dollar savings can really hurt a Six Sigma project. Make sure you and the controller are in agreement on how you define and assign savings to your projects.

Don't skip steps. It may be tempting to try to speed up a project by skipping necessary steps in Six Sigma, but it won't yield the information you need to correct and eliminate the problem in question. Let the data do its job and tell the story—again, we need to stay in the realm of quantifiable facts and not deal in assumptions. You apply statistical measurements and metrics to analyze the issues so that you can prove with data, and not by opinion, why and how you can make lasting changes.

Don't be afraid to learn and use statistical tools. You need to understand and use statistical data and respect its value. Statistics and statistical tools are essential to Six Sigma. However, Six Sigma is not merely a statistical exercise; it employs such measurements to produce undeniable results. You do not need to spend exorbitant amounts of time reviewing stats. With the systems and software available, you'll have the critical formulas and equations at your fingertips, so you can let technology and training work together to yield results. Your implementation partner usually provides such training systems.

Readying the Organization

So now you know what to do and what not do, it's time to figure out how to ready and rally your organization for the Six Sigma journey. It's important and necessary for associates at every level to understand and embrace what you're about to do.

Communicate

Communication is key. Again, the clearest way to signal the importance of Six Sigma and your investment in it is to tell the story as often as you can.

First, use all the tools available, such as your company intranet, newsletter, or other communication channels. Post information on what, how, and when you plan to kick off your Six Sigma projects and publicize the roles and responsibilities of every person participating in the process. State clearly the purpose of your projects: outline the outcomes expected and communicate how the entire company benefits from your efforts.

As discussed earlier, another key element to initiating Six Sigma is to have the unqualified endorsement of senior management. You can communicate this through vehicles like e-mail and corporate newsletters, but you should also take it a step further and find a way for your company leaders to directly address employees. Use videos, company meetings, and the like to get the message out—your executives will be indispensable to getting company-wide buy-in. By the consistent and continual reinforce-

Introducing the Six Sigma Initiative

An effective method for kicking off Six Sigma is a letter of introduction by the CEO or president that's distributed to every employee, to communicate the importance of Six Sigma and executive commitment to its success. Figure 4-1 provides a sample letter, to adapt to your situation.

ment of their support, you can reduce fear of change and inform employees about how they are a part of the success or failure of what you're doing.

From: (President, CEO, or other executive staff member)
To: All Employees
Subject: Six Sigma Success

Today, the world in which we compete is far different from what we've previously experienced. Competition is stronger than ever, customers have more choices and are demanding higher quality and faster delivery, and profit margins are shrinking across our industry. To thrive and effectively compete in this kind of environment and deliver on our commitments to ourselves, shareholders, and customers, we need to explore new ways to improve our performance. There has never been a better time to develop a strategy that will widen the gap between our company and competitors, meet our customers' expectations, and ultimately boost our bottom line.

That strategy is Six Sigma. Six Sigma is the best way for us to break through to the next level of cost savings and delight our customers by rapidly accelerating and improving our performance, processes, products, and services. Our goal is to be a high-growth company and our first target is to become a $_____ company.

The term "six sigma" is actually a measurement that will tell us how rapidly we are eliminating waste and defects in our processes. Yet it is far more than a mere measurement. Building on our existing quality systems, Six Sigma is the way in which we will take our productivity and profitability to the next level.

You will all have the chance to get acquainted with and receive essential training in the Six Sigma methodology. In addition, some people will receive further training and begin to initiate its methods to start achieving our goals. The focus at all levels will be to generate productivity, which is directly tied into our bottom-line performance. Six Sigma will require us to refocus and reformulate both our belief system and our process steps. I urge you to support, endorse, and use its tools to make our company the highest-quality, lowest-cost provider of goods and services in our industry. As we reach our goals, you will be recognized and rewarded for your dedication to the initiative's success.

The executive staff is committed to the program and has already had training on the methodology. We will continue to train participants at all

Figure 4-1. Sample letter of introduction for Six Sigma

levels and will begin Six Sigma "black belt" training on (date). Black belts are the designated project leaders who will assemble teams and begin Six Sigma projects in various areas. We are not going it alone; we have selected (company name) as our business partner. Their expertise, training, and guidance will best position our Six Sigma initiative for success.

Again, your commitment, support, and understanding of our Six Sigma goals are critical. Together, we can achieve the results we're seeking and improve our performance. Please join me in supporting this exciting effort.

Thank you.

Figure 4-1. Sample letter of introduction for Six Sigma, continued

Survey Your Knowledge Base

Once you've expressed your expectations about Six Sigma throughout the organization, it's time to *survey your knowledge base.* Surveying your knowledge base is as individual as your company culture. Every organization is different in terms of how prepared its personnel are to use six sigma tools and begin to manage the data.

Six Sigma can stand alone and still get results, but there are fundamental requirements and foundational training aspects to its process management tools that are necessary. You need to accurately survey your company's knowledge, to identify the gaps or misconceptions and determine how you can best provide training in the methodology to ensure correct implementation. Most important of all is to find out what your black belt candidates know about Six Sigma.

When surveying your knowledge base, you can find out the extent of understanding of Six Sigma by asking your people if they are familiar with any of the following statistical tools, which are essential components for implementing Six Sigma. Once you know how much they know, you can best prepare for their training experience. (We'll discuss these tools in Chapter 7.)

- **Checksheet:** This is a list of check-off items that permits quick and easy collection of data in a simple, standardized format. It's a basic, vital tool.

- **Histogram:** This is a bar chart displaying the frequency of data in subgroups or categories.
- **Brainstorming:** This is a method of getting people together to openly exchange ideas and solutions for specific problems or opportunities. All suggestions are recorded in the meeting's minutes, for possible use immediately or later.
- **Process mapping:** This is a graphical view of your process steps for a given situation. As mentioned in Chapter 3, you map the steps with boxes that show the work process in its entirety, with inputs and outputs for each aspect documented. It gives you an exact insight into a process flow.
- **Pareto chart:** This is a bar graph breaking down a problem into the relative contributions of its components, named for Vilfredo Pareto, the Italian economist who originated the 80/20 principle. It identifies the *vital few* elements that form 80% of the problem, so you can focus on them and ignore the remaining 20%.
- **Run chart:** This chart displays any given measurement over a specified time sequence.
- **Cause-and-effect (fishbone) diagram:** This diagram is used to identify and classify causes of a given effect.

Once you and your staff fully understand these tools and their value, you can use them to identify the defects and waste in your processes.

Assess Your Readiness for Six Sigma

As I've repeated throughout these first few chapters, you must have data for Six Sigma to succeed. Do you have any basic measurements in place for your various business functions? Does your organization collect reliable data in a structured manner?

Whatever you're doing or planning to do, it's important that your information be accurate and credible. Also, you have to be able to define success for every step in every process, so you can determine what constitutes a defect or an error. And you need to know where you stand in terms of your Six Sigma readiness. The checklist (Figure 4-2) is a resource that can help you quickly assess your readiness.

If you agree with the following statements and can answer the questions, you may already be on the Six Sigma journey.

1. Customers have critical-to-quality expectations. Can you list your customers' top four expectations?

    1. _____

    2. _____

    3. _____

    4. _____

2. We are in business to achieve a phenomenal customer satisfaction rate that exceeds critical-to-quality expectations. Can you quantify your customers' current level of satisfaction?   Yes ___ No ___

    If yes, what is it, on a scale of 1-10? _____

    How has it changed over the last five years? _____

3. We strive to produce profitable bottom-line results. We are in business to make money!

    List your company's profits for the last five years:

    Year 1 $ _____

    Year 2 $ _____

    Year 3 $ _____

    Year 4 $ _____

    Year 5 $ _____

4. We have repetitive processes in our business that create products and services for our customers.

    List four major repetitive processes in your business:

    Process #1 _____

    Process #2 _____

    Process #3 _____

    Process #4 _____

    How many times do you do these processes per year?

    Process #1 _____

    Process #2 _____

    Process #3 _____

    Process #4 _____

5. In our processes the goal is to create knowledge and take action to reduce cycle time, defects, and variations.

Figure 4-2. Six Sigma readiness checklist

For Processes #1 and #2 listed above, give the cycle time and the rate of defects or yield (as discussed in Chapter 2).

	Cycle Time	% Defects or Yield
Process #1 Baseline:	_____	_____
Process #2 Baseline:	_____	_____

6. We create knowledge about our processes by collecting data and stating the problem in statistical terms, such as the mean and standard deviation of the process.

   Does your company know the vital statistics of Processes #1-4 listed above? Yes __ No __

7. We validate the data collected through the Measure phase of the Six Sigma DMAIC model. Is your data validated? Can it be trusted? Yes __ No __
   Can you test the data for repeatability and reproducibility by others? Yes __ No __
   Is the data accurate and precise? Yes __ No __
   If yes, then what are the results of the test? _____ % R&R (repeatable and reproducible)

8. We use the data to determine the vital few factors that are the root of the quality problem through the Analyze phase.
   For Process #1 what are the vital few factors?
   Factor #1: _____
   Factor #2: _____
   Factor #3: _____

9. In the Improvement phase, we create a predictable equation or relationship between the process variables (vital few) and output of the product with a low defect level (the Six Sigma equation mentioned in Chapter 3).
   Can you calculate a result equation for Process #1? What is $Y = f(X)$? _____

10. In the Control phase, we sustain the reduction in defects while always quantifying our bottom-line result.
    If Process #1 is in the Control phase, what are the controls?
    What is the financial result of the project? $_____
    You should show the money benefit!

Figure 4-2. Six Sigma readiness checklist, continued

11. We share our knowledge to ensure that everyone understands and benefits from that knowledge.
How does your company transfer knowledge?
What velocity is involved in that knowledge transfer?
Is there an infrastructure in place? (i.e., intranet or database sharing?)

12. We as a company achieve our goals, which results in sustained and satisfied internal and external customers.
What are the goals that have been met in the last two years?
Goal #1 _____
Goal #2 _____

Were you able to understand and answer every question? If no, then your company is an excellent candidate for doing Six Sigma!

Figure 4-2. Six Sigma readiness checklist, continued

Planning

Once you've determined that you're ready to start Six Sigma, you need to know how to plan for it. There are certain phases in Six Sigma planning that serve as the foundation for any implementation; in each phase, there are certain steps that build sequentially to launch your projects.

Communication and Education

As noted earlier, one of the best ways to build awareness about Six Sigma is through a company-wide communiqué from your CEO or president. This sets the tone and the expectation for all employees that Six Sigma depends on everyone's support, regardless of their actual involvement.

Once that has been done, Six Sigma is further introduced in key sessions to executives and managers to reinforce their understanding and support. Beyond that, executive training should be offered to all senior managers and champion training should be offered to managers at all levels.

Executive training should include an overview of Six Sigma, a review of case studies, related product and service demonstrations, deployment strategies, and exploration of scientific tools and methods, statistical analysis, improvement, measurements, and management controls.

Champion training provides the managerial and technical knowledge necessary to plan and implement Six Sigma and mentor black belts. The goal is to transfer and reinforce fundamental Six Sigma strategies, tactics, and tools necessary for achieving the breakthrough in key processes. Training covers the principles, tools, and applications of Six Sigma, including deployment tactics and strategies for establishing metrics, selecting black belts and projects, and implementing Six Sigma.

After introducing Six Sigma to executives and managers and determining who will receive executive and champion training, the next steps in this planning phase are to order training materials, select black belt candidates, and schedule training.

Identification of Projects

During this time, you also start to select your projects. You should be familiar enough with your processes to identify the chronic issues that your Six Sigma teams should investigate and improve. Your outside consultant should support you in selecting the projects that will have high impact on quality and customer satisfaction and will deliver bottom-line savings. You should also identify departments and people that you'll need for support of your projects. (Chapter 8 is devoted to selecting Six Sigma projects.)

Infrastructure

As you compile your list of black belt candidates, you develop "job descriptions" for their new roles and coordinate with your human resources department to post them. Human resources should also benchmark compensation plans that reward black belts and their teams upon the completion of projects.

Once you've selected your black belts, determined how they will be rewarded, and decided what your projects will entail, it's time to kick off the training phase. This involves coordinating all logistics for the training sites, ensuring that you and your executive team are ready to serve as champions and that your training materials and instructors are ready to go. Then, you communicate with black belts about the training schedule and prep them for their first day of class.

Your aim in training black belts is to create technical leaders, advanced users, and teachers of Six Sigma. They should learn its philosophy, application tactics (including statistics, benchmarking, process-control techniques, diagnostic methods, and experiment design), and group dynamics. Then, once you've trained your black belts, you assign them to the projects you've selected. (We'll discuss their roles and responsibilities in Chapter 5.)

Critical to the success of your black belts is the on-site support of an experienced master black belt, usually provided by the outside consultant. A master black belt will guide and coach the black belt candidates and work with champions to help overcoming barriers and obstacles. A master black belt also builds relationships with company leaders to inform and educate them on the progress of their Six Sigma initiative. (We'll further discuss the master black belt in Chapter 5.)

There are also periodical senior reviews. These are formal meetings involving you, other champions, senior leaders, and your outside consultant to discuss the progress of your Six Sigma initiative. The primary purpose of these sessions is to ensure that your teams are meeting your objectives and that the initiative is staying on track.

Implementation Partner

These planning stages can be considered as the steps necessary to laying the foundation for Six Sigma. Each Six Sigma deployment follows essentially the same success model for implementation. The specifics of your particular situation, the projects you select, and the champions and black belts will determine how you create a plan and a schedule for all activities.

In case you're wondering how all of this gets done, remember that your outside consultant is there to direct, train, and execute the critical elements of the planning process. Your implementation partner can help you orchestrate all responsibilities, roles, and schedules to make a smooth transition from planning to implementation.

What to Expect from Outside Consultants

In this chapter, I've talked a lot about "outside consultants" and "implementation partners." Obviously, I am one of these. So now you're thinking, "OK, here comes the sales pitch." Well, yes and no. Let me elaborate on why you should select an outside consultant to help you start with Six Sigma and how to make the most appropriate choice.

First, you need to work with someone who preaches *and* practices Six Sigma. When you're talking about implementing a strategy that's going to change not only your outcomes, but also your processes and the deployment of your people, you'd better get it right the first time. You need to choose an outside partner with a demonstrated track record of being a real "money miner" for client companies. After all, you want your investment to pay off as fast and as effectively as possible. Your consultant should help you lay the groundwork and set up the required infrastructure so you can move toward self-sufficiency quickly.

The consultant should be focused on knowledge transfer, on showing you how to solve problems through the most effective methods and fix process defects with the right tools, so you can transfer that knowledge throughout your organization.

Are They in the Same Boat?

A quick way to distinguish among outside consultants is to look at how they structure their own employee reward systems. We all need to make money, of course. But here's a big difference. Some consultants are rewarded for *time*, on the basis of their billable hours. Others are rewarded for *results*, on the basis of the speed and size of the client's return on investment. Both groups of consultants are committed to your success in theory, but only the latter consultants are in the same boat as you, rowing toward the same objective—financial results.

Finally, when choosing an outside consultant for Six Sigma, check credentials. There are lots of organizations out there purporting to be Six Sigma experts, so you need to sort out fiction from fact. Ask for proof of their claims: request references and actual case studies from bona fide clients. You don't want anecdotal discussion; you want to see the actual linkage to the clients' outcomes. You want proof of results—after all, that's what Six Sigma is all about.

Manager's Checklist for Chapter 4

❑ As you get started, keep your objective clear, stay on track, and focus on results.

❑ Make sure you and your executives regularly communicate why, when, and how you are undertaking Six Sigma projects so that everyone in the organization is committed to your efforts.

❑ Survey how much you and your people actually know about basic Six Sigma tools, to gauge the extent and depth of training you will all need before getting started.

❑ Plan your Six Sigma initiative well. There are many steps to organize and many players to prepare and coordinate, to ensure the best possible outcomes.

❑ Choose an outside consultant with the demonstrated qualifications to best lead your Six Sigma initiative.

Roles and Responsibilities

Whenever you see a successful business, someone once made a courageous decision.
—Peter Drucker (1909-)

It takes courage to decide to do Six Sigma. It takes courage to implement it, to use the Six Sigma techniques and tools, to persevere, to make changes. You can't find that courage in a methodology; you have to encourage and promote it in the people who use Six Sigma.

The success of Six Sigma relies on the people who are responsible for implementing it. Repeat that simple statement as you read through this chapter. Six Sigma provides some powerful techniques and tools, but success depends on the people who play the primary roles and assume the central responsibilities for putting those techniques and tools to work for your organization. Dennis Sester, senior vice president of Motorola Service, has put it very succinctly: "Six Sigma is not a product you can buy. It is a commitment."

Six Sigma necessarily upsets the status quo. After all, if you say you're doing Six Sigma, there's going to be a major interruption—or even an uproar—as job descriptions are redefined and activities are radically changed. This must happen to make any real, permanent changes. Six Sigma cannot be managed on the sidelines; it's a full-contact sport that sets new rules and aims for much higher scores! Everyone is a player, regardless of individual company positions.

However, it's important to point out here that not everyone is slated for full Six Sigma responsibilities. You have to choose well who will run your projects, participate on teams, and pursue the objective using various Six Sigma tools like metrics and other statistical measurements. You need the right mix of the right talents to refocus on Six Sigma projects.

Key Players

So who are the key players and what are their roles? Basically, there are five:

- **Executive leaders:** to commit to Six Sigma and to promote it throughout the organization
- **Champions:** to fight for the cause of black belts and remove barriers
- **Master black belt:** to serve as trainer, mentor, and guide
- **Black belts:** to work full-time on projects
- **Green belts:** to assist black belts part-time

It's vital to understand and define key operational roles from the start. All the key players should know what's expected of them and how all of the roles work together in the Six Sigma initiative. Each of the roles has a clearly defined set of responsibilities.

Executive Leaders

The key role of executive leaders is to decide to do Six Sigma and, as we mentioned in Chapter 4, to publicly endorse it

throughout the organiza-
tion. Company leaders
must kick off and reinforce
the comprehensive scope
of Six Sigma to engage
everyone's support and
participation. It's important
for Six Sigma to be a company-wide initiative: that
point cannot be over-
emphasized. And as you
begin this business-chang-
ing enterprise, visible leadership is crucial. It rallies

> ### Prerequisite: Responsibility
> **Smart Managing**
>
> Regardless of the designat-
> ed role each participant plays in the
> Six Sigma initiative, they must all have
> full responsibility for their individual
> areas. Simply put, to be responsible is
> to be accountable, trustworthy, and
> dependable. It's important that all
> your participants recognize this as
> their charter: from green belt to
> executive, they need to exercise
> responsibility in all that they do to
> achieve optimum outcomes.

the employees, it lends legitimacy to your projects, and it sends
the clearest signal that Six Sigma and your targeted outcomes
are major company priorities.

But what exactly do the responsibilities of executive leaders
entail? There are a few essential aspects that help build and
round out the foundation for successful executive leadership
responsibility.

Determination. For starters, they need to show *determination.*
They need to be resolute in believing that Six Sigma will succeed. So after the initial fanfare of introducing Six Sigma, executives should be determined to get the training, understand the
savings, perpetuate the use of metrics, showcase black belt
achievements, mark key milestones, and keep the overall initiative on track.

As mentioned in Chapter 1, Jack Welch, the CEO who started Six Sigma at General Electric, called Six Sigma "part of the
genetic code" of future leadership at that company. Welch could
be considered the ideal executive leader for Six Sigma, because
an executive's responsibility, ultimately, is to make sure that Six
Sigma becomes part of the "genetic code" of the company.
From the top down and throughout all points in the organization,

executive leaders can inspire and promote a Six Sigma culture that continually produces results.

Confidence. Executives need to actively display confidence—not only in the Six Sigma method, but also in the people charged with making it work. By actively showing their confidence with rewards and incentives, company leaders inspire sustained commitment and effort on the part of employees. When an executive lets employees know that he or she believes in them, supports their success, and applauds their talents, employees will respond in kind. Confidence is a powerful motivator.

And bear in mind that confidence isn't all compliments and congratulations. It can be supported by the facts and figures that emerge from project metrics; executives can point to specific outcomes and prove that confidence in a given champion, black belt, or project team has been validated. As the old saying goes, "It ain't bragging if you can do it."

The Compensation Link

General Electric has encouraged its executives to promote Six Sigma by linking it to compensation: 40% of the bonuses for the top 7,000 executives is tied to Six Sigma implementation. That incentive sends the message about the importance of Six Sigma and ensures commitment from the top levels down.

Integrity. Executives must back it all up with integrity. *They need to do what they say they're going to do.* This inspires ever-increasing confidence among project teams that an executive's word is good and that there's substance behind the statements. By following through on commitments and staying true to a stated purpose, executives demonstrate a high standard of ethical leadership. Integrity stimulates loyalty and respect, both of which are motivators for employees across the organization.

Patience. Executive leaders are responsible for practicing and modeling patience. This may seem obvious, but it's very hard to do in a business environment that demands instantaneous results and immediate answers. Six Sigma projects take time;

Progress Ahead: Drive Slowly

If a company has been functioning at a four sigma level or lower for the last decade, then surely company leaders can allow six months for projects that will bring its performance up to a six sigma level. That seems logical—but too often executives and managers are impatient for results.

Your department may be operating from month to month in terms of its profitability and everyone may be anxious for improvement, but you've got to ask how much of the problem you want to fix—all of it or just some of it? To fix it properly, you and your executive team need to invest the time to do it right—and that takes patience!

---

skipping steps or rushing the process will jeopardize the results.

Company executives have a golden opportunity to develop their relationship with employees when they demonstrate their determination, confidence, integrity, and patience. By "walking the walk" as well as "talking the talk," they stand out from the crowd and they show that Six Sigma is far more than the latest trendy business theory. Executives send the signal that they're actively engaged in leading and facilitating exciting changes in the organization and that they fully support the employees driving those changes.

Champions

Champions are critical to the success or failure of any Six Sigma project. The concept of "champion" dates back to the Middle Ages, to a word for field or battleground. A champion was someone who took the field to battle for a cause. In Six Sigma, a champion is an advocate who fights for the cause of black belts and to remove barriers—functional, financial, personal, or otherwise—so that black belts can do their work.

Champions are closest to the process and it's not an exaggeration to say that they "own" it in every respect. Depending on the size of a company, champions are drawn from the ranks of the executives and managers. Champions have responsibility for the daily oversight and management of each critical element. They need to report up to senior management about project progress and they need to support their teams. Champions must be sure that the projects they select align with the executive strategy and can be readily understood and embraced by project teams.

Champions select black belt candidates, identify project areas, and establish clear and measurable goals for projects. They do whatever it takes to keep the projects on schedule.

They must be fully engaged in the process, allotting at least 20% to 30% of their time to ensuring that black belts are making progress on their projects and effecting lasting changes. It's the job of the champion to identify and remove obstacles so that the black belt can continue to focus on their projects and achieve the bottom-line outcomes. You can't do that from the sidelines; champions must be in the thick of the battle!

The champion acts as advocate and defender, as mentor and coach. The champion is ultimately responsible for the Six Sigma project. The black belt and project teams are on the hunt for defects and waste, but it is the champion who selects the

---

What Makes a Good Champion?

At a manufacturing company implementing Six Sigma, a designated champion regularly met with his black belts. At one report-out meeting, a black belt informed him that she needed to purchase and install a table for sorting defects off-line. It would cost about $17,000, but it would provide an alternative to shutting down the entire line, which would cost far more. The controller told her to go through the normal requisition process and she'd have her table in about four months. That delay would have killed the project right then and there: to submit the project to "business as usual" would have shown little real commitment to supporting Six Sigma. So the champion asked for the data that backed up her request, analyzed it, agreed with it, and then got immediate executive sign-off on securing a table the following week.

This is the stuff of a good champion: removing barriers and sending a clear signal that he and upper management are aligned and committed to Six Sigma. The champion does whatever it takes to support the black belts.

project and monitors its performance. Champions must thoroughly understand the strategy and discipline of Six Sigma and be able to educate others about its tools and implementation. Champions direct and mobilize the teams to make lasting change. They also ensure that the teams share what they learn; they transfer the knowledge into other areas and increase the results exponentially.

In reading this book, you are taking a very important first step as a Six Sigma champion.

Master Black Belt

This role is often fulfilled initially by a member of your implementation partner's team. The master black belt serves as your trainer, mentor, and guide. He or she teaches you the ropes, helps you select the right people, and assists in screening and selecting projects that will best achieve the hidden dollars you are after.

Once you have your Six Sigma initiative well under way, once you've established all necessary elements, designated and trained people in their roles, started projects, and garnered some results, you can graduate members of your teams to the ranks of master black belts. This ensures not only the survival of your initiative, but its sustained success. Six Sigma initiatives must be self-perpetuating; as your team members gain experience and some become master black belts, you're well on your way to sustaining Six Sigma results.

The master black belt is an expert in Six Sigma tools and tactics and a valuable resource in terms of technical and historical expertise. Teacher, mentor, and lead agent of change, the master black belt ensures that the necessary infrastructure is in place and that black belts are trained. They focus 100% of their efforts on process improvement.

A key aspect to the master black belt role is the capacity to skillfully facilitate problem-solving without actually taking over a project. In this way, you and your team members have the security of knowing that you've chosen the best project, that you're correctly using the tools, and that you will find the hidden streams of waste—all without losing autonomy, responsibility, or the ability to direct change.

A master black is an invaluable asset as you begin your Six Sigma initiative—coordinating and collaborating with you and upper management, advising and coaching black belts, and ultimately keeping you—the champion—focused on what's important in selecting projects and implementing Six Sigma.

Black Belts

Black belts work full-time on selected projects. As team leaders and project heads, black belts are central to Six Sigma success. They are trained to dig into the chronic and high-impact issues and fix them with Six Sigma techniques and practices. It sounds quite simple; they fix the problems, get rid of the defects, and find the money.

The black belt role is one of great responsibility and discipline and, as defined in Chapter 1, it is the backbone of Six Sigma culture. Black belts move theory into action. Following the steps introduced in Chapter 1—Define, Measure, Analyze, Improve, and Control—black belts sort out the data, separate opinion from fact, and present in quantifiable terms the vital few elements that are causing productivity and profitability problems.

Although champions are responsible for getting the bottom-line results, since they select the projects and monitor progress, black belts are responsible for doing the work. They relentlessly pursue the project objectives, they strive to understand the causes and effects of defects, and they develop the necessary steps to permanently eliminate them. They are selected to solve problems within the Six Sigma framework and they are trained to be technical leaders in using Six Sigma tools and methods to improve quality.

They are at the core, working the projects with a 100% dedication to fixing chronic costly issues. They make sure that what gets improved *stays* improved! Black belts manage risks, help set direction, and lead the way to quantum gains in product or service quality.

Green Belts

Green belts assist black belts in their functional area. They work on projects part-time, usually in a limited, specific area. They apply Six Sigma tools to examine and solve chronic problems on projects within their regular jobs. In this way, knowledge is being transferred and used in even narrow applications.

They also help black belts accomplish more in less time. They may help collect or analyze data, run experiments, or conduct other important tasks in a project. They are team members with enough understanding of Six Sigma to share the tools and transform company culture from the ground up. Working in a complementary fashion with the charter of executive leadership, champions, and black belts, green belts are essential "worker bees" driving bottom-line results.

Selecting Black Belts

As we've discussed, black belt projects are central to Six Sigma, with important responsibilities as technical experts, team leaders, and project heads. A champion must take great care in designating black belts. So, how does a champion select employees for this role?

First of all, not every employee is a black belt candidate. It's a full-time discipline that combines leadership ability, technical skills, some statistical knowledge, the ability to communicate clearly, and motivated curiosity. If you know the members of your staff, their skill sets, and their performance, you can accurately determine who might be a good candidate. The sidebar, "Rating a Black Belt Candidate," provides an organized approach to evaluating your employees in terms of their black belt potential.

Black belts are the technical leaders and change agents, the key players who implement the Six Sigma principles, tech-

> ### Rating a Black Belt Candidate
> Here's a quick way to evaluate a potential black belt. Rate the employee in each of these 11 key areas, on a scale of 1 to 5 (5 = excellent, 4 = above average, 3 = average, 2 = below average, 1 = unacceptable).
>
> Process and product knowledge _____
> Basic statistical knowledge _____
> Knowledge about your organization _____
> Communication skills _____
> Self-starter, motivated _____
> Open-minded _____
> Eager to learn about new ideas _____
> Desire to drive change _____
> Team player _____
> Respected _____
> Results track record _____
> Total: _____
>
> A candidate who scores at least 38 has excellent black belt potential.

niques, and tools. Successful black belts generally share the following traits:

- They work well on their own and also in groups.
- They remain calm under extreme pressure.
- They anticipate problems and act on them immediately.
- They respect their fellow workers and are respected by them.
- They inspire others.
- They are able to delegate tasks to other team members and coordinate their efforts.
- They understand and recognize the abilities and limitations of their fellow workers.
- They show a genuine concern for others, for what they need and want.
- They accept criticism well.
- They are concerned about the current processes and results and they want to improve the system.

- They have the intelligence and interest to learn how to apply the Six Sigma tools.

Choose your black belt candidates carefully. It takes certain qualities to be a black belt; training develops these qualities, but it can't create them. You want to maximize your return on investment in every way, so it's essential to choose the right people for these roles that are central to Six Sigma.

Manager's Checklist for Chapter 5

❑ Your primary resources are your people, particularly the ones who will play the key roles in your Six Sigma projects.

❑ Understand and define key operational roles from the start. All the key players should know the responsibilities of their roles and how all of the roles work together.

❑ Involve executive managers in leading the Six Sigma initiative and in promoting it throughout the organization. Their leadership is critical to success.

❑ Champions must own the process in question and be dedicated to doing whatever it takes to make it easier for the black belts to achieve results.

❑ Use the expertise and experience of a master black belt wherever and whenever you can. These outside, skilled practitioners can be extraordinarily valuable in helping you get your initiative under way.

❑ Select black belt candidates with care. Training can develop the essential qualities, but it can't create them.

The Core of Six Sigma

Deviate an inch, lose a thousand miles.
—Chinese proverb

Now you know about the Six Sigma roles and responsibilities, here's the heart of the matter—the steps for doing Six Sigma. Like the proverb says, even a small deviation in a process can have big consequences. Deviation, variation, defects, or waste—whatever you call it, the end result is the same: it costs you! No matter your business—manufacturing, distribution, or other services—any hidden waste streams in any of your processes ultimately siphon off dollars that should be going to your bottom line.

As you implement the core Six Sigma methodology, you will be armed with the tools that enable you to identify, correct, and control the critical-to-quality (CTQ) elements so important to your customers and reduce the cost of poor quality (COPQ). (The tools that we don't explain here we'll cover in Chapter 7.) Once you start implementing the method full-time with your black belts and project teams, your projects will start revealing costs that are hidden and returning that money to the company!

The DMAIC Method

The acronym DMAIC represents the five phases in the Six Sigma methodology:

- Define
- Measure
- Analyze
- Improve
- Control

(As noted in Chapter 1, sometimes the methodology is applied without a Define phase. I prefer using a four-phase MAIC sequence, but you should be familiar with the five-phase DMAIC sequence as well.)

I like to refer to MAIC as "magic without the 'G' for 'guess-work,'" as it is capable of creating and sustaining remarkable, data-driven results that continually boost your profitability levels. MAIC/DMAIC is the key to the Six Sigma problem-solving method; in fact, it's fair to say it *is* the problem-solving method.

Like virtually everything else you do in Six Sigma, DMAIC/MAIC involves necessary steps in a sequence, each of which is essential to achieving the desired outcome. You can't skip or jump around with the four or five phases and expect to get credible results. There's no value in starting with Control, for example, and working your way back to Measure or Define. By following each step in the

---

CAUTION!

Focus on Facts
It's worth remembering that, as you begin to implement DMAIC, everything in the Six Sigma world can be reduced to an equation. In other words, no matter what you're looking at or what you think about the way a given process operates, you can develop a statistical analysis that will evaluate its performance in quantifiable terms, free from opinions and emotions. Six Sigma is about facts, not opinions—you can't measure perceptions, but you can evaluate equations!

order and completing the tasks for each, you can accurately understand, evaluate, and work on all aspects of the CTQ
elements influencing the given process answer.

Six Sigma Problem-Solving Sequence: Define, Measure, Analyze, Improve, Control

Define Phase
  1. Identify the important problems in your processes.
  2. Select a project to combat one or more of the problems and define the parameters of the project.
  3. Determine the vital few factors to be measured, analyzed, improved, and controlled.

Measure Phase
  4. Select critical to quality (CTQ) characteristic(s) in the product or process; e.g., CTQ Y.
  5. Define performance standards for Y.
  6. Validate measurement system for Y.
  7. Establish process capability of creating Y.

Analyze Phase
  8. Define improvement objectives for Y.
  9. Identify variation sources in Y.
  10. Screen potential causes for change in Y and identify vital few X_i.*

Improve Phase
  11. Discover variable relationships among the vital few X_i.*
  12. Establish operating tolerances on the vital few X_i.*
  13. Validate measurement system for X_i.*

Control Phase
  14. Determine ability to control vital few X_i.*
  15. Implement process control system on vital few X_i.*

*Note: X_i = initial X's.

Figure 6-1. The five phases of Six Sigma DMAIC

So there you have it, the logic behind the four or five phases
and an outline of the steps within those phases. As you know
from the preceding chapters, Six Sigma involves a lot of statistics
and equations—but don't let it throw you. Six Sigma is not merely
a statistics program; rather it shows you how to use statistics and

how to understand their value, in order to make rational and measurable decisions about your business processes.

Our goal is not to produce reams of statistics; it is to produce six sigma outcomes and reveal hidden revenue streams you might otherwise never discern. Statistical measurements and metrics are the key to finding those hidden opportunities.

D—Define Phase

It's important that you start Six Sigma by clearly defining the problem. That's the purpose of the define phase.

You first must define the chronic "big" issues in your department or organization. It's often useful to map processes, in order to better understand them and locate the problems.

Then you select a project to combat one or more of them. It's critically important that you define parameters of the project. You need to scope out the project and understand at the outset what you want to accomplish with it. Understanding its scope and sequence exactly defines your project's rules—how long it will run, what you're examining, your goals, and the tools and personnel in place to achieve them.

Next, you hand over the project to your black belts. They will build the project team to further scope out the CTQ elements and then start solving the issues.

Even though any project necessarily is a "limited" event, don't limit the quality of your results by not fully knowing its scope and goal criteria. The more you know, the more likely you are to find what you're looking for.

Central to the Six Sigma methodology is the use of a key equation that defines which vital few factors need to be measured, analyzed, improved, and controlled for bottom-line results. As defined in Chapter 1, the vital few factors are those factors that directly explain the cause-and-effect relationship of the process output being measured in relation to the inputs that drive the process. Typically, there are a half-dozen or fewer factors that most affect the quality of outputs in that process, even if there are hundreds of steps in which a defect could occur.

> **TRICKS OF THE TRADE**
>
> ### The Vital Few Equation: Y = f (x)
>
> As you use MAIC/DMAIC, you'll quickly realize that it depends on the precision and accuracy of statistical analysis and mathematical formulations to succeed. Chief among these is the vital few equation: $Y = f(X)$. So what does it mean?
>
> Y is the outcome of a process; it is a function of X's, the key variables (the vital few factors) in a process. Y is the characteristic of quality you're trying to achieve. By identifying the X's, you can measure, analyze, improve, and control them to achieve optimal results in the shortest time. By funneling all process elements through the equation, you will get to the vital few factors that best predict the outcome. Once you have a predictable outcome, you can make the changes that reduce your costs. Basically, the equation lets you identify what you didn't know—and that's the power of Six Sigma knowledge in action.

When you identify these factors, you can concentrate your efforts where the impact and return are greatest.

Defining the project is the first step in the Six Sigma method. You can now move into actually fixing the problem with the remaining four phases of the method.

> **TOOLS**
>
> ### Define Phase Deliverables
>
> Each DMAIC phase has key deliverables that you must complete and then use as documented, quantified evaluations for a project. For the Define phase, basic deliverables include the following:
> 1. Project status form
> 2. Metric graph
> 3. Process map with tally points
> 4. Pareto charts
> 5. Improvement plans/next steps
> 6. Local review

M—Measure Phase

When you start the Measure phase, you first must identify the crucial internal processes that influence the CTQ measurements, which are the Y's, the process outcomes. Once you know what they are, then you can measure the defects generated in the process that profoundly affect the CTQ standard.

So, for example, if your customer expects a certain standard at a certain price, you need to identify the vital few factors that affect that expectation. This is crucial, since determining the vital few allows you to concentrate your efforts and resources. Then you must measure the impact of defects in those areas. As you recall from Chapter 1, defects are measurable characteristics of a process or its output that are not within the acceptable customer limits or specifications.

Once you identify the defects, you can then ask how much money you would save if they were eliminated. In doing so, you are immediately connecting your project work to a dollar impact—relating improved quality with improved profitability. There is a direct and measurable relationship between defects and dollars. In the Measure phase, you can figure out that relationship exactly.

The Measure phase is completed when a black belt can successfully measure the defects generated for a key process that affects the CTQ characteristic. In the Measure phase, the black belt conducts a measurement systems analysis, which includes *gauge studies*, and a thorough evaluation of the capability of the process.

The purpose of a gauge (or gage) repeatability and reproducibility study (gauge R&R) is to ensure that your measurement systems are statistically sound. A gauge R&R measures how you're measuring, so you know that all aspects of your measurement systems are functioning properly and that you're getting maximum value for your efforts. After all, you're going to be investing a lot in rooting out the problems that your measurements reveal, so it makes sense to be sure that they're accurate and appropriate.

A gauge R&R consists of a series of steps. They encompass calibrating your actual gauge for measurement, having various team members conduct tests on random samples in a number of trials, and finally assessing the statistical data for soundness. Essentially, the study plays two roles:

- It can alert you to any discrepancy within defined measurements, so you can correct them at the beginning of projects, rather than discovering your data is flawed months later.

- It can validate that what you're doing is credible, that you're using metrics that not only make good sense, but also will get you the information you need to reduce or eliminate defects.

Gauge R&R repeats measurements under various conditions to test the measure against these four essential criteria:

Gauge repeatability and reproducibility study A study to ensure that your measurement systems are statistically sound. The gauge (or gage) R&R is a confidence meter of sorts! It measures how you're measuring, so you know that your systems are measuring accurately and appropriately.

- **Accuracy.** How precise is the measurement?
- **Repeatability.** If the same person and/or piece of equipment measures the same item more than once, will the results be the same?
- **Reproducibility.** If other people and/or other pieces of equipment measure the same item, will the results be the same?
- **Stability.** Will accuracy, repeatability, and or reproducibility change over time?

Gauge R&R studies enable black belts to determine whether or not their data is accurate, repeatable, reproducible, and stable—qualities essential to making any progress at all in improving a process. (In some cases, your measurement analysis will show that you might be better off flipping a coin rather than using inherently flawed data! We're reminded of that old joke about clocks, the instruments we trust to measure time. The clock that's unreliable is less to be trusted than the clock that's broken—because the latter is right twice a day.)

The Measure phase is all about mapping the process, evaluating the measurement system, using your metrics, and estimating the process baseline capability. It's truly complete when your black belts can identify the vital few factors (X's), demon-

The Star Kicker

Smart Managing

In Chapter 3, I introduced you to the field goal kicker to demonstrate the interplay of the terms *specification, specification limits, capability, distribution, baseline,* and *defect.* Now let's take another look at the kicker in the context of DMAIC.

He can kick the ball from 50 yards to distribute it within the 18' 6" space between the two goal posts. However, even though he makes a good percentage of his attempts, he's not consistent, sometimes kicking the ball to the left or right. He wants to concentrate on placing his kicks through the exact middle of the goal posts, so any shift won't put his kick outside the posts.

He needs to know what Y (accurate kicking through the center) is a function of. He needs to ask questions like "What's the angle of the ball on the ground? What is the force of my kick? How high is the initial trajectory? What's my follow-through eye and leg position?" Once he asks and answers such questions, he knows and can measure the vital few factors and take the steps necessary to control and improve his kicks for 100% precision, 100% accuracy, 100% of the time.

strate the capability of the process, and establish a valid measurement system.

Measure Phase Deliverables

TOOLS

Each DMAIC phase has key deliverables that you must complete and then use as documented, quantified evaluations for a project. For the Measure phase, basic deliverables include developing:

1. Project status form
2. Metric graph
3. Process map with tally points
4. Pareto charts
5. Measurement tools, including gauge R&R studies
6. Improvement plans/next steps
7. Local review

Once you've assembled this documentation, you'll have the critical information in hand that points to exactly what and how you measured your project to isolate the vital few factors that are so central to your Six Sigma improvement efforts. It's a disciplined approach to validating and plotting the entire course of your project.

Now that you and your teams know what the vital few factors are, it's time to move on to the Analyze phase.

A—Analyze Phase

At this point, you try to understand *why* defects are generated and then break down what multiple reasons (again, the X's) are identified as causing them. Put another way, you and your black belt teams will ask which *inputs* are affecting the *outputs*.

In mapping and measuring your process and identifying input variables that may affect your critical-to-quality attributes, you've probably come up with some assumptions about relationships between your business metric (your critical-to-quality defect measurement, the Y) and the inputs (the factors, the X's) that would affect it. So, now you formulate hypotheses and statistically test them to determined which factors are critical to the outcome.

This is where the Analyze phase becomes a cycle, as you go through a series of hypothesis testing. The cycle consists of the following steps:

1. Develop hypothesis about cause(s).
2. Analyze process and/or data.
3. If the hypothesis is correct, add cause(s) to the list of vital few. If the hypothesis is incorrect, refine it and go to Step 2 or reject it and go to Step 1.

Hypothesis testing uses a series of detailed analyses to calculate the probability that the factors that you've identified as the vital few truly have most important impact on the critical-to-quality outcomes. You then move from your statistical conclusions to devising practical solutions, developing plans for taking corrective action.

Key Term **Hypothesis testing** Investigating a theory about the suspected cause(s) of a particular effect in a process to determine if it is correct. It's a compass that points you directly to the vital few factors that are most affecting your process.

Analyzing the Loan Application Process

Let's say the loan application process considered in the first three chapters runs two shifts to handle the transactions. Shift One has far fewer delays, less rework, and faster funding of its loans; in other words, it has far fewer *defects*. Shift Two, in contrast, is riddled with paperwork mistakes, processing delays, and other defects. If you can get Shift Two to perform like Shift One, just imagine the profitable possibilities! This is where the DMAIC method comes into play.

What do we know? We know that the overall loan process has capability, judging from Shift One, but defects are limiting its performance, judging from Shift Two. What are the vital few factors that cause the difference in performance between the two shifts?

We need to map each shift's process steps to figure out where the deviations occur. When you compare both shifts statistically, you can measure the differences, analyze the differentiating factors, and bring Shift Two up to the standard of Shift One.

When you and your project teams are in the Analyze phase, you are continually brainstorming in a statistical sense—you are challenging the status quo and really looking into what vital few factors are influencing the outcome of a given process, eliminating the trivial many to reveal the significant few.

Once you have a clear sense of the vital few factors that are likely to cause the majority of variation, you are ready to go on to the next phase, Improve.

I—Improve Phase

After you've carefully (sometimes painstakingly!) measured and analyzed the situation, you arrive at the exciting point of actually testing your theory to find an equation to solve the problem. In the Improve phase, you confirm key variables and quantify the effects of those variables on critical-to-quality outcomes (Y's). As a result, you can identify the maximum acceptable range of each variable to ensure that your measurement system can actually measure that variation.

When you reach the Improve phase, you can modify each variable so that it stays within the acceptable range. When you

> ## Analyze Phase Deliverables
> **TOOLS** Each DMAIC phase has key deliverables that you must complete and then use as documented, quantified evaluations for a project. For the Analyze phase, basic deliverables include completing:
> 1. Project status form
> 2. Metric graph
> 3. Tool use as required, to show competence—gauge R&R, Pareto charts, etc.
> 4. Solution (root cause)
> 5. Improvement plans/next steps
> 6. Quantification of improvement plans
> 7. Local project review
> 8. List of significant causal factors
>
> Once you've completed this documentation, you have the critical information in hand that indicates exactly the vital few factors, the rate of the effect of each of them, and the next corrective actions. It's a disciplined approach to determining the course of your project.

can turn a defect on or off to truly improve both sides of the $Y = f(X)$ equation, you can manipulate the vital few factors (X's) to achieve the outcome (Y) you want.

> ## Key Term
> **Variable** A characteristic that may take on different values. There are two kinds, dependent and independent. Their roles are significant in terms of the effect they have in any process.
>
> **Dependent variables** The factors that depend on other factors. For example, in the equation $Y = f(X)$, you can't adjust the dependent variable Y (the outcome); you must adjust the other factors, the X's, to effect change.
>
> **Independent variables** The input factors—the X's—that determine the output factors or the outcomes as a result of their functions. Among these we identify the vital few factors that influence and determine almost every aspect of a process. In DMAIC, these are the elements we work to isolate and then control.

Improve Phase Deliverables

Each DMAIC phase has key deliverables that you must complete and then use as documented, quantified evaluations for a project. For the Improve phase, basic deliverables include expanding on:

1. Project status form
2. Metric graph
3. Tool use as required, to show competence—hypothesis testing, gauge R&R, Pareto charts, etc.
4. List of significant causal factors
5. Solution (containment action)
6. Improvement plans/next steps
7. Quantification of improvement plans
8. Local project review

Once you've completed this documentation, you have the critical information in hand that indicates exactly not only the vital few factors and the rate of the effect of each of them, but also the actions you plan to take to improve or eradicate them. It's a disciplined approach to implementing necessary action to reduce and eliminate the damaging effects of defects.

C—Control Phase

The Control phase is where you maintain the changes you made in the X's in the equation in order to sustain the improvements in the resulting Y's. In this phase, you continue to document and monitor processes via your defined metrics and other measurement tools to assess their capability over time. In some cases, the Control phase never exists, because you eliminate the problem entirely.

Following the logical sequence of DMAIC, the Control phase allows you to maintain a higher level of quality and productivity. By mapping processes and then measuring and analyzing each factor, you know how to improve and control them. These control mechanisms can be both macro and micro in scope.

You now know what you need to do to make lasting, profitable changes. You know what works and what doesn't. Now you have the roadmap for staying on course.

Controlling Lost Luggage Rates

In the airline lost luggage scenario, various factors play pivotal roles in determining the probability of your bags accurately arriving at your destination. For example, misrouted luggage can be caused by errors at the check-in counter, mislabeling of bags, inattentive loading dock staff, or even something as seemingly insignificant as sharing a printer. Here's what I mean.

When labeling luggage, two operators use the same printer at the check-in desk. They get busy, long lines form, and they have to work faster. What happens? As they both print and pull off tags, each inadvertently takes the other's tags, so your luggage is destined to be lost from the start!

Once an error such as this is identified through the MAIC process, the airline can take the necessary corrective step of investing in separate printers for each operator. The additional printers will more than pay for themselves within days: after all, how much does it cost to reroute luggage incorrectly labeled? The lesson is clear: control the process, control the outcome!

Control Phase Deliverables

Each DMAIC phase has key deliverables that you must complete and then use as documented, quantified evaluations for a project. For the Control phase, basic deliverables include finalizing:

1. Project status form
2. Metric graph
3. Specific control/validation plans
4. Verification of improvement/results in metrics and dollar savings
5. Significant lessons learned
6. Final report
7. Local project review

Once you've completed this documentation, you have the critical information in hand that indicates exactly not only the vital few factors and the rate of the effect of each of them, but also what you're going to do specifically to sustain the gains you've made. It's a disciplined approach to staying the improvement course that's already under way.

The Power and Discipline of the Sequence

The DMAIC/MAIC method takes you away from a mentality of
"I think," "I feel," or "I believe." As I mentioned earlier in this
Chapter, I like to refer to MAIC as "magic without the 'G' for
'guesswork.'" DMAIC/MAIC relies on measurable facts to root
out waste and inefficiency. It's the ultimate tool set for lasting
quality improvement, validated by bottom-line results. It's the
core of the Six Sigma problem-solving method. By teaching you
a step-by-step discipline that defines, measures, analyzes,
improves, and controls the variables that determine the value of
your outcomes, DMAIC/MAIC is the key that unlocks true Six
Sigma success for your business.

Manager's Checklist for Chapter 6

❑ Six Sigma is based on the MAIC/DMAIC method, a four- or
   five-phase process: Define, Measure, Analyze, Improve,
   and Control.

❑ MAIC/DMAIC relies on the equation, $Y = f(X)$: Y is a function of X. This means that every outcome of every process
   is a function of the inputs.

❑ In the first phase, Define, you identify the important problems in your processes, select a project and define its
   parameters, and determine the vital few factors to be
   measured, analyzed, improved, and controlled.

❑ In the second phase, Measure, you study and evaluate all
   steps in your process, mapping the key indicators—the
   vital few factors that determine your outcomes.

❑ In the third phase, Analyze, you work with all the information gathered in the Measure phase to determine potential
   causes and to prepare for making key changes to positive-
   ly alter each scenario.

❑ In the fourth phase, Improve, you can take corrective
   action to reduce or eliminate the negative effects of the
   identified vital few factors. This is where managers, black

belts, and project teams get the positive results of their careful investigation and quantification of process mapping.

❑ In the last phase, Control, you "sustain the gain," focusing on maintaining the improvements you've made to your processes. It establishes the roadmap for future productivity, for monitoring and ensuring that your changes are consistent and permanent.

Quick Overview of Six Sigma Tools

*Good management consists of showing average people
how to do the work of superior people.*
  —John D. Rockefeller (1839-1937)

The overall Six Sigma methodology is implemented by using a specific set of statistical tools throughout each phase. These tools are the keys to unlocking the information that will yield the answers you need to improve performance. They are focused, specific, and sequential. They address and quantify the narrowest margin of error and the broadest action plan.

Management Roles

As you plan, train for, and execute your Six Sigma initiative, it's important to remember where you fit in the scheme of things. You've selected your black belts who are leading the tactical charge of your projects and you've assembled the project teams to ensure their efforts are carried out. So where does this leave you?

As both the manager and champion of the project, you are in a unique leadership capacity. You can motivate and inspire your people and ensure that they stay on track, on time, and on target with projects by being an accessible, active, and strategic advisor. Nowhere is this more apparent than when statistical tools come into play—you need to rally the critical participants, analyze their investigations, provide feedback on the results, and, above all, keep the path clear and the goal in sight.

As I pointed out in the Preface, you don't need to become a statistician or develop the expertise of a black belt, but you need to know the basics about the fundamental tools used in Six Sigma methodology. For each of the tools in each of the MAIC/DMAIC phases, your presence is essential. The black belts and the team members will turn to you for assurance, support, and guidance in reading the data and deciding what to do with that information as you build your Six Sigma case. It's exciting, challenging, and ultimately rewarding as you and your project team use Six Sigma tools to return untold dollars to the bottom line!

Your Tool Map

Taking the Six Sigma journey requires a map. It's made up of a set of specific analytical tools that direct the course of all your efforts and point you to the path you need to follow to improve your processes. Within the MAIC/DMAIC method and your projects (which you'll select in Chapter 8), there are sequences of tools. Some of these tools may seem complicated, but we'll cover the essentials. Also, some of these tools will be useful in more than one phase.

And, like everything else we've discussed, you can't just start wherever you like and expect results. Six Sigma follows a pattern; it may seem overwhelming at first, but once you've done it and you realize the power of its precision, you'll see the big-picture benefit.

Warm-up Tools

The first tools you're going to use are what I call "warm-up" tools. At the beginning of your project, you're going to conduct initial investigations into a specific process. The key types of tools to use as you begin are basic statistics, graphical analysis, and simple correlation studies. The warm-up tools help you begin to understand and represent data obtained from measuring a process.

To help us run through

> ### Keep It Simple
>
> Sometimes the best tool for an important task is the simplest. That's often the case for the checksheet, which we introduced as "a basic, vital tool" in Chapter 4.
>
> A checksheet is a form, usually a matrix, for collecting data quickly, easily, and efficiently. For our call center example, we might list the 20 operators down the left side of the matrix and indicate across the top the time increments—one minute or less, between one and two minutes, between two and three minutes, and so on. Then, whoever is monitoring the calls could simply time each call and then put a tally mark or a check in the proper cell.

these tools, we'll use a simple example. Our situation: you manage a call center and you want to look into the time it takes operators to handle incoming calls. You track the times for 20 operators to each handle 10 calls. That gives you 200 *data points*. The times vary widely: eight minutes, three, 10, and so on. Now what?

Basic Statistics: Mean, Mode, and Median

You start understanding your 200 data points with some basic statistics. We begin with three simple calculations that we presented at the beginning of Chapter 3 to better understand data: mean (average), mode, and median. These are basic statistical tools for dealing with data.

Mean. The *mean*, as you'll recall, is the sum of a series of values divided by the number of values. Statisticians often call it more specifically the *arithmetic mean*. Regular folks usually call it the *average*.

The mean answers the first question you ask about your call
center: how long does each call take on average? You add up
the 200 data points and divide the total by 200, to determine
that the average time is 10 minutes. You can then decide what
your response time objective should be and then devise ways to
achieve that objective.

Figuring out the average of a group of data points isn't hard;
in fact, it's quite simple. But it's fundamental. Each tool builds
on the preceding one. You start with the basics and build your
case for improving your processes.

Mode. To give us another perspective on our 200 data points,
we can calculate the *mode,* which is the value that occurs most
often in our sample. We could learn, for example, that the mode
is seven minutes, which could be evidence that it's possible to
set an objective for reducing all calls to seven minutes.
Unfortunately, the mode could be a time anywhere along the
spectrum. For example, we could find that 30 calls took only
one minute—but that there were 29 calls that took seven minutes and 29 that took 12 minutes. So, maybe the mode doesn't
tell us much about our data.

Median. The next basic statistical tool for understanding your
200 data points is the *median.* That's the midpoint in our series
of data points. We just line up our 200 times from lowest to
highest and find the value midway between the lowest and the
highest. Ideally, we might expect the median to be about the
same as the mean, about 10 minutes. However, a dozen very
short or very long calls in our group of 200 sample calls could
make the median lower or higher than the mean, so our median
could be eight minutes or 12 minutes.

After we've done our basic statistical equations, we may
want to use some graphical analysis tools

Graphical Analysis

The warm-up tools in this group represent data graphically, so
you can analyze patterns and interrelationships. A key warm-up
tool for graphical analysis is the *histogram.*

Histogram. A histogram is a group of vertical bar graphs that shows the distribution of one variable in a group of data. The histogram reveals patterns in performance, taking us beyond mean, mode, and median, which measures what's known as the *central tendency* of a group of data. (Because the histogram is a good tool for early analysis, it may also be used in the Define phase of DMAIC.)

> **Histogram** A group of vertical bar graphs that shows the distribution of one variable in a group of data. The histogram visually represents all of a set of data points on a two-axis graph, to show the *distribution* of all those data points and to reveal patterns. Also known as a *frequency distribution bar chart.*
>
> *Key Term*

Here's how we can use a histogram to represent the 200 data points in our sampling of calls. You make a two-axis graph. Along the horizontal axis you plot your call times in *bins*—under one minute, between one and two minutes, between two and three minutes, and so on. (The increments that we call bins here are also called segments, groups, classes, or buckets.) Along the vertical one axis you indicate frequency: zero calls, one call, two calls, and so on. (This is why a histogram is also known as a *frequency distribution bar chart.*)

Then, for each of the time bins, you draw a bar that shows the number of calls that took that long (Figure 7-1).

The histogram visually represents the *distribution* of all your 200 data points—how many one-minute calls, how many two-minute calls, etc. It also reveals patterns. For example, there might be a lot of calls between three and six minutes, for example, and very few between seven and 12. Or the calls might show what's considered a *normal distribution*, in the shape of a bell, with the highest point in the middle and smoothly and

> **Distribution** The organization of the data on a graph. From the distribution, you begin to turn data into usable information.
>
> *Key Term*

symmetrically sloping away from the center on both sides.

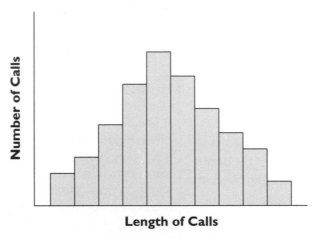

Figure 7-1. An example of a histogram

An important consideration in displaying data in a histogram is *bin width*. In our example, the time bins were set in one-minute increments. We could make them smaller—as small as the exactitude of our measurements will allow. Since the longest call in our sample of 200 was 22 minutes, we can stick with 22 one-minute bins or plot 44 half-minute bins or even set up 88 bins in 15-second increments. Smaller bin sizes might allow us to detect distribution patterns that are not evident with our one-minute bins.

The histogram adds a new aspect to your investigation—the *distribution* of elements in your process. Not all distributions are normal. When the slopes are not symmetrical, when the curve on one side is longer, the distribution is said to be skewed. Sometimes a curve has two peaks. But we won't get into these abnormal distributions here in our overview.

Distributions are not just for statisticians. Here are two examples of distribution familiar to most of us. Think about where people sit at a baseball game. People usually want to sit near home plate; once those prized seats are taken, people take seats along the baselines toward first and third. So the distribution of spectators usually clusters around home, then stretches out toward the sides. Or think about trying to find a good parking space at the mall. Most people prefer to park near one of the doors. So, you see the heaviest distribution of cars clustering around the doors, with the rest of the cars stretching out from those choice parking areas. If you took an aerial photograph of the baseball field or the parking lot, you'd likely see the bell-shaped curve characteristic of normal distribution.

So now you know how to calculate means, medians, and modes and you know a little about distributions of the data points gathered by measuring your process. You're ready to move on to dispersions. We use a different measurement for those—because now we've entered the variation zone!

The important thing to remember about variation is that your customers "feel" it. Take, for example, our call center. We know the average is 10 minutes; if a call takes much longer than that, say 15 minutes, your customer is going to feel the effects of the spread of the data, which is vari-

> **Key Term**
>
> **Dispersion** The degree to which values for a variable differ from each other. If every value for a variable were close, the variable would have very little dispersion. Also known as variability and spread.

Variation

At the beginning of this book, I used the example of a fast-food order mix-up to demonstrate what six sigma performance really means. Now, let's revisit it in the context of understanding variation.

You're in the drive-through lane, waiting to pull up to the window to get your order. You have to wait a certain amount of time, because there's an average time to service each order, depending on what it is. You expect that. But when you get to the window and an employee tells you, "Please pull up front and wait," you feel the effects of variation, which you don't expect. You sit there waiting for your order and watching other people get their orders and leave.

How about your customers? If they feel the weight of your process variations, they'll remember and have a negative perception of your service or product.

ation. (And it won't feel good!) When an operator takes 15 minutes or longer to take care of a call, you can tell the customer that your average call time is 10 minutes—but it probably won't make the customer any more satisfied with your service.

When we calculated the mean, the mode, and the median above, we were measuring the *central tendency* of our data. To measure the *dispersion* of data, we can calculate *range, variance,* and *standard deviation.*

Range. As you may recall from Chapter 3, the range is simply a measure of the spread of data points, the difference between the highest value and the lowest value. Let's go back to the call center histogram. What's the lowest bucket of time and what's the highest? If our shortest and longest calls were one minute and 22 minutes, the range would be 21 minutes. That figure shows that there's a lot of spread in the call-answering process. However, it doesn't tell us enough.

That's why we use the two other common ways to measure dispersion—*variance* and *standard deviation.* They provide more accurate and meaningful information about the dispersion of our data points, by measuring how the data points for a process spread around the mean of the data set.

Variance. To calculate the variance of a data set, calculate the mean of the data points, measure the amount by which each point deviates from the mean, and then square that deviation.

Numerically, the variance equals the average of the several squared deviations from the mean.

> **Key Term**
>
> **Variance** A measure of the amount by which a value differs from the mean, calculated as the average squared deviation of each number from its mean.

OK, that may be a little confusing. But if you understand that variance tells you more about dispersion than range and you can use statistical software, then you're ready to go.

Standard Deviation. You can then take your analysis one step further to determine the *standard deviation* of the process, a concept that you may recall from Chapter 3. To calculate the standard deviation, you take the square root of the variance.

The standard deviation is, in simple terms, the average distance from the mean, or how far off the average of the variance is from your middle ground. The standard deviation is the most commonly used measure of spread. It can be readily conceptualized as a distance along the scale of measurement—unlike the variance, which is a somewhat abstract measure of variability.

Another means of discovering patterns in a graphic form is the *run chart* (also known as a *line chart*) (Figure 7-2). Run charts are used to analyze processes according to time or order and reveal patterns that occur over time.

> **Run chart** A graph that plots performance data over time for a process, representing the data usually as a line chart. It presents and compares numeric data, indicating changes over time with a line connecting data points.

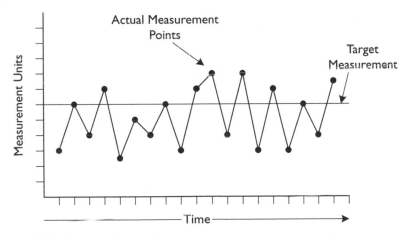

Figure 7-2. A typical run chart

Simple Correlation Studies

The third leg of the stool of warm-up tools is a correlation study. *Correlation* is an overworked and incorrectly used word that gets tossed around in business a lot. Correlation as a statistical concept is the degree to which variables are related. For factors to correlate, there must be a cause-and-effect relationship, not just a coincidence. The input must affect the output. As one goes up, the other goes up—correlation describes direction as well as linkage. (However, it's important to keep in mind that correlation does not necessarily mean causation.)

A correlation study is used to quantify the relationship, if any, between two sets of data points. The typical graph used in a correlation study is a *scatter plot* (or *scatterplot*) (Figure 7-3). A scatter plot provides a good visual display of the relationship

> **Key Term**
>
> **Correlation** The degree to which two variables are related, measured in terms of a *correlation coefficient* (between 1 and −1). Correlation does not necessarily mean *causation*.
>
> **Scatter plot** A graph in which individual data points are plotted in two dimensions. Also known as a *scatter diagram* or a *cross plot*.

between the two sets of data points. To create a scatter plot, the possible values for one data set are marked along one axis and the possible values for another data set are marked along the other axis.

If the data points plotted on the graph cluster to form a diagonal line running upward from left to right, the data would be showing a positive correlation coefficient. In that case, whenever one variable has a high value or a low value, so does the other: the correlation coefficient is 1. At the other extreme, if the

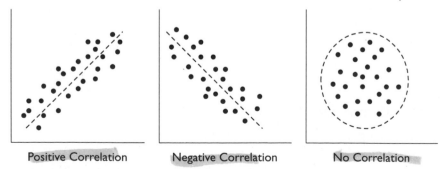

| Positive Correlation | Negative Correlation | No Correlation |

Figure 7-3. Scatter plots show positive, negative, and no correlation between two factors

> **Correlation coefficient** A number between -1 and 1 that measures the degree to which two variables are linearly related. If the two variables have a perfect linear relationship with positive slope, the correlation coefficient is 1; if there is positive correlation, whenever one variable has a high value or a low value, so does the other. If the two variables have a perfect linear relationship with negative slope, the correlation coefficient is -1; if there is negative correlation, whenever one variable has a high value, the other has a low value. A correlation coefficient of 0 means that the variables have no linear relationship.

data points show no correlation, the correlation coefficient would be 0.

First Steps

With all the warm-up tools, you take the critically important first steps of finding out fundamental information about a process, including the average and the spread of data, and then understanding cause-and-effect relationships. Those steps serve as the building blocks for all the rest of your corrective Six Sigma actions. Once you have mastered the basic warm-up tools, you can choose from a selection of more advanced, key tools that will be essential as you track down defects and quantify them in hard, scientific terms.

Key Tool #1: Process Mapping

Your first key tool is process mapping, a concept presented in Chapter 3. Used during the Measure phase of DMAIC/MAIC (and during the Define phase as well), process mapping is an integrally important tool that helps you understand every aspect of every input and output. It helps you document the process so that you can maintain control and reduce variation due to changes over time.

Process mapping steps are very simple but extensive: you've got to list all the inputs and the outputs (all the steps, all the cycle times, etc.). It's fair to say that in general everything has a process attached to it—there are inputs and outputs, distribution and variation occurring in virtually any scenario you can think of. As you get under way with process mapping, you start identifying the value-added and the non-value-added factors inside the steps. You list and classify each step in this context—digging deeper and deeper to ensure that you've documented absolutely every factor affecting each step in that process. Once you know all the inputs and factors, you can then designate them as external or internal and determine whether their effect is good or bad. You can then layer on operating specifications and ask about the targeted specs for the particular process.

In a nutshell, a process map is a "living" document: it helps you document the process so you can maintain control over what you change and be alert for variations as they start to pop up over time.

The key fundamental of process mapping is to develop an accurate, comprehensive pictorial of the entire process system. The standard tool is a flowchart, a schema to show operations, decision points, delays, movements, handoffs, rework loops, and controls or inspections. By breaking down the process into steps, the flowchart simplifies analysis of the process. As you map your process, it's equally important to ask two key questions: for every step, you must ask why you do it and how you know it's good.

Managers can use process mapping to serve as a check-and-balance system for reaching the desired outcome. Process maps keep critical team members and resources focused and involved and help them identify the benefits and opportunities of attacking the bottlenecks, capital constraints, or other material problems. They can also be ultimately used proactively to remove barriers.

Key Tool #2: The XY Matrix

Welcome to the "House of Quality," as the XY matrix is also called, another tool for use in the Measure phase. That's because the XY matrix is used to link your customers' critical-to-quality (CTQ) requirements to your process inputs, to ensure you have the right set of priorities in your process-improvement activities.

> **XY matrix** A group of rows and columns, with one set of increments marked along the X (horizontal) axis and another set of increments marked along the Y (vertical) axis. Also known as an *x-y matrix*.

How? By taking a highly structured approach to brainstorming.

Brainstorming

Brainstorming is a method for generating ideas. Participants focus on a problem or an opportunity and come up with as many ideas as possible and push the ideas as far as possible.

During brainstorming, there is no criticism or discussion of any ideas; the point is to generate ideas and expand thinking about the problem or opportunity. As participants mention their ideas, somebody records the ideas on a board or a flipchart. (If the focus is on causes of a problem, the cause-and-effect diagram described below is useful for keeping track of ideas.) Participants can build on each other's ideas.

Then, after brainstorming, the team can analyze the results and explore the best ideas. Brainstorming is also a valuable tool for probing during the Analyze phase and for generating ideas during the Improve phase.

Cause-and-Effect Diagram

This graphical tool can be used to identify the relationship between a problem and possible causes of the problem. The structure resembles a simplified fish skeleton, hence another name for this tool, the *fishbone diagram*. (It's also called the Ishikawa diagram, because it was popularized by Kaoru Ishikawa, a pioneer of quality management processes.)

The primary branch (spine) represents the effect and is typically labeled on the right side of the diagram, as the head of the fish. Each major bone branching out from the spine corresponds to a major cause or class of causes. Minor bones branching off from major bones correspond to more detailed causal factors. This type of diagram is useful in any analysis, as it illustrates the relationship between cause and effect rationally.

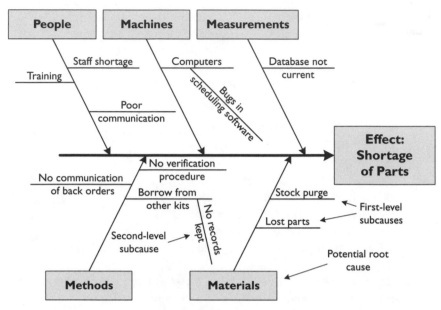

Figure 7-4. An example of a cause-and-effect diagram showing causes for the effect, shortage of parts

What I mean is that you and your project team can list the inputs for the particular process and then compare them with a list of outputs that are really important to your customers. The purpose for using the XY matrix is to study and understand the relationship between what you're putting into a process and what your customer is getting out of it. The XY matrix allows the team to identify gaps, areas for improvement.

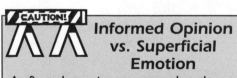

Informed Opinion vs. Superficial Emotion

At first glance, it may seem that the XY matrix is contradicting everything you've learned about Six Sigma so far, because it's based on opinion, not fact. But the important thing to remember here is that the opinions are *informed*: the matrix is based on the team's expertise and on thoughtful, constructive group analysis of the issues.

So you develop a matrix that demonstrates that *Y is a function of X*: you line up the process inputs (the X's) against the process outputs (the Y's that are functions of those inputs) (Figure 7-5).

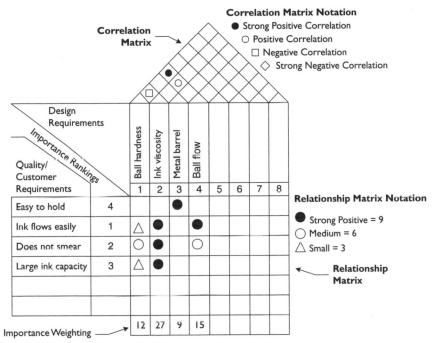

Figure 7-5. An XY matrix (house of quality) showing a simple example of a ballpoint pen and the connection between design and customer requirements

What's a Good Cup of Coffee?

The hotel coffee service example presented in Chapter 2 illustrated how differently providers and customers can view critical-to-quality (CTQ) factors. This is where the XY matrix can help.

First you list the output variables—in this case taste, aroma, price, and acidity—and then you rate them on the scale from one to 10. For example, taste and aroma would be a 10, but acidity would probably be only a two (or somewhat higher for customers with sensitive stomachs). So you've narrowed down key customer CTQ factors to taste and aroma.

Then, you rate your key input variables—which include coffee type, amount, grind level, water temperature, brew time, and cup type and size—against the output variables. This time, you can get at some solid information, such as the relationship between coffee type and taste and aroma. Since taste and aroma are huge CTQ factors, there's a direct correlation between coffee type and taste and aroma, which gives your project team the information it needs to start fixing the process.

(There's that simple formula again: $Y = f(X)$. Output Y is a function of Input X.)

Then the members of the team rate the inputs on a scale of one to 10 in terms of their importance to the customer. Next, you then rate the input variables against the output variables using the same scale, based on the relationship between X and Y. You end up with a blueprint of the input factors that most affect the outcome, what your customer wants.

With the XY matrix, you're trying to prioritize what people think and believe about a given situation. Then, you can go and collect data that will validate those beliefs. Again, it's not about guessing; it's about disciplined thinking on customer priorities. The XY matrix is a directional tool; it points out what you think are the suspect variables in a process so you can start measuring them.

As in process mapping, a manager's role is to ensure the active involvement of team members, remove barriers, serve as a check-and-balance for the outcome, and be certain that the team's consensus on key data actually represents the customers.

Key Tool #3: Measurement Systems Analysis

Measuring Your Measurements

Think of the measurement systems analysis as taking the measure of your measures, to make sure that your measurements are good. By testing what you're testing, you can ensure that your data are sound and you can keep on track to eliminate the cost of poor quality in your process. If you don't know that your measurement's right, then how can you know that your solution is right?

The goal of the third key tool is to ensure that your measurement system is statistically confident—that it's both accurate and precise each and every time it is used. Undertaken during the Measure phase, your measurement systems analysis (MSA) determines whether or not you can take a certain measurement and repeat or reproduce it among different people who take the same measurement. You want to be sure all your measurement systems function independently and correctly 100% of the time; otherwise, you risk flaws in your data.

Within the MSA tool is another specific tool, the gauge repeatability and reproducibility study, which compares your measurement devices against others. The gauge R&R study, presented in Chapter 6, ensures that you're measuring what you think you're measuring. It looks at your units of measure and number of variables, calibrates the measurement gauge, and then randomly selects samples to measure against different operators. Once all the trials are completed, the study shows where the flaws are and takes corrective action.

Your role here is to involve all team members and to expedite any action necessary to correct your measurement systems, as the project cannot move forward without it. Again, to maximize the considerable investment of time and resources involved in a Six Sigma project, you've got to be sure that you are measuring the right stuff in the right way to get the right results.

Key Tool #4: Process Capability Tool

As you come to the end of the Measure phase in MAIC/DMAIC, the last tool you deploy is vitally important. Process capability,

---

Rush Hour

It's Monday morning and you're off to work. What's the average time it takes you to get to work? If you give yourself 10 minutes to get there, are you *capable* of doing that every day? Yes—barring accidents, excessive traffic, road construction, and stopping for coffee. But, realistically, over time these and other factors are going to affect, if not determine, your capability of meeting your 10-minute commute specification. By conducting capability studies and graphing the probability of performing to the given specification, you can see what adjustments you need to make in order to get to work on time, every time, despite usual and even unusual outside influences.

as defined in Chapter 1 and explained in Chapter 3, is the measure of a process being able to meet specification requirements and fulfill customer CTQ needs on a long-term basis. It's great that you can identify, measure, and fix something immediately, but to really reap the benefits you must make that fix last. You remember our field goal kicker? He was capable of putting the ball through the uprights, but over time his accuracy had faltered and his kicks veered left and right. That's why we use capability metrics: to find out whether or not we're going to hit the target without variation over time.

Again, through a series of steps, process capability analysis establishes short- and long-term deviation patterns and baseline performance for each process. The tools determine whether or not the process is performing within the specifications, show you how to decrease variation, and help you chart the direction necessary to reach optimum, statistically proven capability.

> **Pareto chart** A representation of the relative importance of process causes or defects, based on the rule of thumb originated by the Italian economist Vilfredo Pareto, that 80% of all problems result from 20% of the causes (known as the *Pareto principle* or the *80/20 principle*).

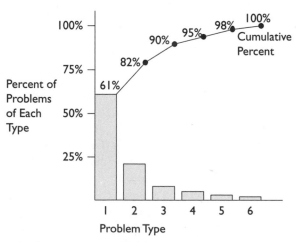

Figure 7-6. An example of a Pareto diagram showing percentages of different types of problems occurring on a job

When you understand process capability, you also understand how to control it. Here again you ensure that all team members are involved, you remove barriers, and you expedite solutions. As long as you know what the study's findings mean in terms of business benefits, you can take the steps to achieve them.

Pareto Chart. One way of graphically showing the relative importance of causes, defects, and other aspects of a process is through a Pareto chart. The chart graphically represents an application of the Pareto principle, presented in Chapter 4. The axiom introduced by Vilfredo Pareto, the Italian economist who originated the 80/20 principle, holds that 20% of a group of agents or factors account for 80% of the results. In terms of Six Sigma, this rule of thumb generally means that 80% of problems result from 20% of the causes.

You can use Pareto charts to identify factors in a process that have the greatest cumulative effect, so you can focus on a few important factors. You plot each factor, from most important to least, in descending order of relative frequency. Then, the most essential factors stand out graphically.

The Pareto chart is valuable for analyzing a process. We'll get into specifics when we use it in Chapter 8 to select a Six Sigma project.

Key Tool #5: Multivariate Study

As you begin the Analyze phase of MAIC/DMAIC, you may use multivariate studies to identify the significant inputs and characterize the process. You need to know how the inputs affect the output capabilities of the process. Multivariate studies look at sources of variation

> **Key Term**
>
> **Multivariate study** An analysis that offers a way to reduce possible causes of variation in a process to a family of related causes, by graphing the interrelationship of multiple variables. The multivariate chart presents an analysis of process variation by differentiating three main sources: intra-piece (variation within a piece, batch, or lot), inter-piece (additional variation from piece to piece), and temporal (variation related to time).

within a piece or a batch, variation from piece to piece, and variation related to time to discern which one contributes the most to
that variation. They characterize the process baseline capability
while in production mode to collect the data. The data is then analyzed to determine the capability, stability, and relationships
between key inputs and outputs. Once done, you can identify the
inherent capabilities and limitations of the process. Multivariate
studies compare how the same functions, performed by different
people or in different shifts, perform over time.

In your role, you continue to manage the participation of the
team, seeking out full involvement, removing barriers and expe-
diting solutions. By managing in this way, you will be the first to
know which are the vital few variables of variation and be able
to direct short-term containment as you figure out long-term
solutions.

Key Tool #6: Hypothesis Testing

As you continue in the Analyze phase, the next tool at your disposal is the hypothesis test tool. Actually, it's not so much a
tool as it is an approach—procedures for making rational decisions about possible causes of a given effect.

Hypothesis testing, defined and outlined in Chapter 6, statistically compares things to determine a probability value and
isolate the "guilty parties." Through measuring process attributes and capabilities and identifying variables that may affect
your CTQs, you've developed some assumptions or hypotheses
about the process, key variables, and areas to target for
improvement. Now, through a logical sequence of steps,
hypothesis testing defines the problem, statistically tests data
assumptions, selects samples, and determines whether or not
the probability of defect is caused by random chance or has a
more tangible cause hidden in the process.

One of the ways to test hypotheses is through simulations.
Software programs allow you to plug in data and conduct "what
if" tests to apply your hypotheses.

As the project continues, so does your management of this tool, for you repeat your role in keeping team members involved, removing barriers, and knowing what the test results are producing to keep the focus on gathering data in the short term to develop long-term solutions.

Key Tool #7: Failure Mode Effect Analysis

Failure mode effect analysis (also variously known as failure mode effects analysis, failure mode and effect analysis, and failure modes and effects analysis, but most generally by the acronym, FMEA) takes place during the Analyze

> **Key Term**
>
> **Failure mode effect analysis (FMEA)** The manner in which a part or process can fail to meet a specification, creating a defect or non-conformance, and the impact on the customer if that failure mode is not prevented or corrected.

phase. Once you've collected the data, you must know how failure modes affect customer CTQ. FMEA is a disciplined procedure that allows you to anticipate failures, identify them, and prevent them. It's a method for designing in reliability while minimizing causes of failure. Simply put, preventing failure modes prevents defects.

There are risks associated with defects and it's vital to know about those risks. The FMEA process asks about the cause of a defect, its effect, and the probability of the defect occurring. Since the customer impact can be immense, it's essential to know and understand both

> **For Example**
>
> **Failure Mode Implications**
>
> It's important to remember the possible or probable snowball effect of even a small failure mode. As defects go undetected, each defect affects at least one subsequent action. As the effects accumulate, performance is further undermined and the associated risk priority increases. When you fail to detect and document a failure mode trend, the consequences can reach far beyond customer dissatisfaction. In the automotive or aerospace industries, for example, any failure mode can literally have life-or-death consequences.

ends of this cause-and-effect relationship to fix it.

Further, the FMEA asks if you can detect the defect and assess its severity. Defects can range from nuisance to catastrophe. The FMEA assesses defects and their relative risks in a structured format.

FMEA charts the type of defect, severity of defect, probability of occurrence, and whether or not systems are in place to properly detect it. The FMEA then assesses a "risk priority" number to the defect, to rate the severity and urgency of that defect. (This is why FMEA is sometimes known as FMECA—failure mode effects and criticality analysis or failure mode, effect, and criticality analysis.)

In your capacity as the managing champion of this project, you need to know the study's findings and all the implications to understand the risks. You can use the FMEA to correct each and every failure mode as you direct your team.

Key Tool #8: Design of Experiments

As you reach the Improve phase, you actively seek to adjust various aspects within the process to see what's needed to change the outcomes. At this point, all your data is assembled and you fully understand the implications of the defined failure modes. It's time to start correcting the problems.

With the Design of Experiments (DOE) tool, you do exactly that. It's a powerful tool that helps you identify and quantify the effect of the X's on the Y's. It helps you determine which inputs are significant in affecting the output of a process. It also helps quantify the values of the input variables to meet the output requirements. Using DOE helps you really gain knowledge about your processes and understand them better.

So, what is DOE? It's a means of identifying the

> **Key Term**
>
> **Design of Experiments (DOE)** A way of determining and measuring the importance of two or more factors on the outcome of a process, by experimenting with many factors and variables simultaneously. Also known as *multivariable testing* (MVT).

most influential factors more efficiently than with traditional means. To put it simply, rather than experiment with only one factor at a time, you can experiment with many factors simultaneously.

If, for example, there are five interacting factors to be studied, the traditional approach would require 2^5—32!—experiments to explore all potential interactions among the five factors. If you need to repeat each test several times, the traditional approach takes a lot of time and money. And as the number of factors rises, the costs increase exponentially.

DOE allows you to identify a smaller number of experiments that can measure the interactions more efficiently. A typical designed experiment has three factors, each set at two levels—typically the maximum and minimum values for each of the factors. Such an experiment would require eight runs. After those runs have been completed and the results measured for each run, an empirical model can be built to predict process behavior based on the results for the values of these factors.

DOE consists of 14 steps. They may sound complex, but in reality they're quite straightforward. In general, this is the sequence of activities you need to undertake when you design experiments:

- Define the problem.
- Establish the objective.
- Select the response variables.
- Verify the measurement system for factors and responses.
- Select the independent variables.
- Plan logistics.
- Manage logistics.
- Create setup procedures.

Getting Organized with DOE

The efficiency of DOE pays off if you plan properly. Failing to allocate enough time and thought to formulating the initial experiments often results in wasting resources throughout the rest of the experiment. In most cases, up to 50% of your overall effort should go into properly planning DOE. You must have a good understanding of all the variables and plan how you're going to experiment with them. Once you've planned appropriately, the analysis part is easy!

- Collect data.
- Analyze data.
- Draw statistical conclusions.
- Replicate results (validation).
- Draw practical solutions.
- Implement solutions.

As you lead your project team, it's important to be patient in gathering results and ensure that you allocate sufficient time to conduct and complete DOE. It requires planning to work properly. DOE saves time and resources—if you don't try to cut corners setting it up.

Key Tool #9: Control Plan

You are now in the concluding phase of DMAIC/MAIC, the Control phase. The last tool you use is the control plan, which provides a written description of the system to control parts and processes. But a control plan is far more than a recitation of facts and steps. It improves quality by doing a thorough evaluation of process characteristics and variation sources. It helps to increase customer satisfaction by focusing resources on process and product characteristics that are important to customers. It improves communication by identifying and communicating changes in process characteristics, control method, and characteristic measurement.

A control plan is a detailed assessment and guide for maintaining all the positive changes you, your black belt, and the project team have made. It ensures that all your analysis and efforts stay in effect and that you have the information at your disposal to prevent backsliding or a return to less than optimal performance standards.

One important point to remember here: for Six Sigma to work, the process must be in control. If the process is out of control, measurements such as mean and process capability have little meaning.

What does it mean for a process to be "in control"? Good

question! Ideas and rules differ. But the basis for any understanding of the concept of control is the control chart.

Control Chart. The control chart is the fundamental tool of statistical process control: it indicates the range of variability that's

> **Common cause** An inherent natural source of variation in the output of a process. Also known as a *random cause.*
>
> **Special cause** A source of variation that is both unpredictable and not due to normal causes; it's an exception. Also known as an *assignable cause.*

built into a process (known as *common cause variation*). Thus, it helps determine whether or not a process is operating consistently or if a *special cause* has occurred to change the process mean or variance.

The bounds of the control chart are marked by upper and lower control limits, as described in Chapter 3. The *lower control limit* (LCL) and the *upper control limit* (LCL) mark the minimum and maximum inherent limits of the process, based on data collected from the process. Data points that fall outside these bounds represent variations due to special causes; these causes can usually be identified and eliminated. On the other hand, improvements in common cause variation require fundamental changes in the process.

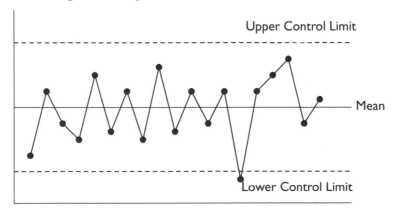

Figure 7-7. A typical control chart (note: one point falls below the lower control limit, indicating a special cause variation)

A process is considered to be in control if all variation is random and if it conforms to the following three basic rules:

- No data points outside control limits
- No runs of 7 data points ascending or descending (evidence that a movement is occurring in the process)
- No trends of 7 data points above or below the mean (evidence that a process has shifted)

Here are some important questions to ask in the Control phase:

- What is the control plan?
- Are control charts being used?
- How will control chart readings be checked to monitor performance?
- Will any special training be provided for control chart interpretation?
- How will the team be able to maintain the gains?
- What key inputs and outputs will the team measure periodically?
- How will the team check input, process, and output variables for conditions that are less than optimal?
- How will the team keep current on changes in customer expectations and use them to improve the process?

In the Control phase, you need to be sure, once again, that all team members are involved. You must also ensure that the control procedure is followed and that there are accountability measures attached to it. Ultimately, you want people to take responsibility for the plan and to take ownership of its lasting success.

Manager's Checklist for Chapter 7

❑ As your team uses the Six Sigma tools, your advisory and leadership roles will be critical to their continued project success. Stay informed about project stages and be ready to understand each data set as the team presents it.

❏ There are nine key sequential statistical and scientific tools used in the Six Sigma methodology. Managers need to know the purpose of each, its relevance, and how to interpret results.

❏ Your role combines both tactical and strategic elements; Six Sigma projects are hands-on, so managerial leadership must be active, flexible, and supportive.

Selecting
Six Sigma Projects

Three-fourths of the mistakes a man makes are made because he does not really know what he thinks he knows.
—James Bryce (1838-1922)

A s your Six Sigma initiative takes off and your black belts are ready to get to work on projects, the big question that remains is deciding how to select projects that will be most successful, that will return the maximum result. There are certain criteria that must come into play when choosing a project. Although this may seem obvious, it's important to remember why you're undertaking the work. It's easy to be enthusiastic and feel ready to apply Six Sigma virtually everywhere you look, but not every business scenario warrants the label of "project."

Once you've narrowed the field and selected projects that best fit Six Sigma and your criteria, you should present your plans for senior-level staff to review and approve. In this way, you get their buy-in and support of the project and they get a clear sense of what the objective is and exactly how you and your black belts are going to pursue it.

> **Not Every Decision Is a Project!**
>
> As you get started with your Six Sigma project teams,
> bear in mind that not every business issue needs to be
> treated as a "project." As good as the methodology is, you don't need
> to use it in every instance.
>
> Here's an example. Your business is consolidating and you need to
> reduce your facilities from two to one. It's not necessary to allocate
> Six Sigma resources, scope the project, and get black belts on the case.
> All you need to do is sell off the extra building and move its assets
> into the other. You don't need to collect any data; you know what has
> to happen. Remember that with a Six Sigma project, you must identify
> a specific problem or set of problems and then solve it with your
> black belts and project teams to capture the hidden revenue streams.

Project Criteria

There are two important criteria for a successful project: the
effort required and the *probability of success*. What do I mean?

First, you must have a good understanding of the duration
of the project in relation to the return on investment. In other
words, it could take more than the project's duration before you
see the money. You have to evaluate your effort in terms of the
resources you deploy (black belts, expenses, etc.) and
the time it takes until those
resources produce for you.

Second, you must con-
sider the probability of success for a project. What
are the risks associated
with being successful? You
need to consider the time,
effort, and implementation
factors to figure out if the
project is desirable.

When considering proj-
ects, it's best not to initiate
a massive undertaking that
is impractical and requires

> **Pick the Low-Hanging
> Fruit**
>
> If you want to fill your
> bushel basket as quickly as possible,
> you pick the low-hanging fruit. The
> same is true of your Six Sigma proj-
> ects. If you want to show results as
> quickly as possible, to build momen-
> tum behind the Six Sigma initiative,
> you aim at the easiest targets.
>
> A rule of thumb is to select proj-
> ects that have a low ratio of effort to
> impact. Basically, you should choose
> projects that fit the criteria of offering
> high-value outcomes for limited effort.

> ### Scoping a Project
> The scope of your project should be manageable, but not so narrow that the solution is already in front of you. If the solution is in front of you and you know it, then you should just do it and don't waste your black belt's time. Keeping your project focused keeps the objective clear and puts all your Six Sigma resources to their best use. Bear in mind that there's a balance.

a lot of time, people, and departments. Staying focused on the core issues and methodically attacking them through a series of projects keeps the objective in sight and a lot more attainable.

Smaller, well-focused projects that target individual process elements can also be leveraged to produce more than one positive result. You should give priority to projects that address one or more factors that are critical to your customer's expectations of quality, cost, and delivery. If you can address all three elements, you can maximize the leverage of your projects in delivering the CTQ standard your customers demand. That's a matter of quantifying the *impact* of each project. You should also quantify the *effort* required by each project. That analysis leads to quantifying the *probability of success*. That's basically a matter of assessing the risks, taking into account such factors as complexity, uncertainty of completing the project, and barriers.

Defect Project Selection Opportunities

Defeating the defects means defeating the cost of poor quality (COPQ), as introduced in Chapter 2. Basically, COPQ is the criterion by which you judge all your potential projects. Projects must have defined cost savings attached to them; otherwise there's no real point to taking them on. Sure, it might sound good and feel good to have improved something, but in Six Sigma the only mark of a successful project is the dollars you've saved and pushed to the bottom line. Since we know defects exist and that there's a measurable cost attached to them, we need to filter out the activities that don't cut costs and concentrate on finding that hidden revenue.

You also need to further refine and pick projects for black belts that exemplify the $Y = f(X)$ equation you learned about in Chapter 3. That equation asks the all-important question, "What is Y a function of?" As Y is the outcome of any given process, you can focus on the vital few factors, the X's determining its quality. This keeps you focused on selecting projects for which you can truly get at the answer with quantifiable metrics.

Project selection should reflect the major issues confronting your business. Your leadership team also needs to know and support your project choices. Any business has three main elements associated with it: sales, profits, and costs. Your projects are designed to attack and reduce or even eliminate costs. Whether you're working in sales, marketing, manufacturing, or other arenas, each and every one of your processes have connected costs. Your job is to root them out and establish a measurement to assess their effects.

First, you must identify and prioritize the suspected sources of issues affecting your critical-to-quality (CTQ) metrics. You then identify the "owners" of the suspected sources (which could include you!), who then become the project champions for those issues. Next, you can get into identifying the Six Sigma methods of improvement to deploy on a particular project. In essence, you make a list.

Now that you have this list, you need to ask these two essential questions:

- Has the project been undertaken before?
- If not, *then will its business benefit outweigh the cost and effort required?*

After you've asked and answered these two basic questions, you can then set a timeline boundary for your project—usually no more than six months. Is the data available to get started with the project? If not, you need to start collecting it to create a baseline. Since in most cases, and especially for transaction-based projects, there won't be any data, you need to develop a data-collection plan. But first, you must create a project problem statement.

Project Problem Statements

Creating a good project statement is one of the hardest things to do in Six Sigma. Your statement must be quantifiable and specific; otherwise, you won't have a clue about what you're actually going to work on. Your statement attacks the business process at its core and looks at the business metrics around it.

There are two purposes to having a problem statement:

- To focus the team on the process deficiency or the actual defect.
- To communicate your project's purpose to "significant others."

Who are these significant others? They are your company's leaders, executive teams, or other high-level personnel to whom you have to ultimately report your findings.

Your problem statement is a boiled-down metric of your project. Through your statement, everyone understands what the problem is and what the benefit will be once your team has fixed it.

Project Objective Statement

You must also address your project's objective. As a corollary to stating what the problem is, you need to indicate how it's

---

Good vs. Bad Problem Statements

Smart Managing   Developing a good problem statement is critical to communicating and directing your project mission.

A good problem statement for a project reads something like this: *"Product returns are 5% of sales, resulting in a profit impact of $5 million and customer dissatisfaction rates in excess of 50%."* The statement is specific: it presents defined numbers illustrating the problem, and indicates the core cost and customer satisfaction issues.

In contrast, a poor problem statement would be: *"Our product return levels are too high due to product A and will be reduced by analyzing first- and second-level Pareto charts."* Why is this problem statement poor? First, because there are no numbers, so there's no quantifying the scope or scale of the problem. Second, all it states is what you're going to do, instead of precisely and accurately addressing the problem.

going to be solved. You do so by following up your problem statement with a strong objective statement that does the following:

- It quantifies the expected performance.
- It indicates the improvement target for that perform-ance.
- It identifies the expected time frame for both the expected performance and the improvement target for that per-formance.

In your project objective statement, you state the following:

- Where you are.
- What you need to do to change the process.
- How long it will take.
- How much money you will save.

Once you've defined the project problem and its parame-ters, it's time to drill down and identify the actionable items within. In what is now a familiar refrain to you, we do this through measuring and analyzing key factors of the project. At this point, we turn to Pareto charts to help us graph and quanti-fy the variables.

Good vs. Bad Objective Statements

An objective statement, like a problem statement, can be derailed by not keeping the focus on what, when, and how much you're going to do to reach the goal.

Smart Managing

A poor objective statement might go like this: "We *will reduce ship-ping errors by implementing individual performance measures and objec-tives."* What's wrong with this? There's no quantification or time limita-tion on how or what is going to be accomplished.

A good objective statement, on the other hand, reads something like this: "We *will reduce shipping errors from 5% to 2.5% of total shipments by this year's end."* This is very specific: it indicates the scope, the goal, and the time it will take to complete the project and reach the objective.

Getting Help from Consultants

A key role for any qualified outside consultant for Six Sigma is to help champions in the project selection process. They should help by assessing the entire business picture and reviewing your profit-and-loss statements, cost of goods sold, annual budgets, and other financials. Their expertise and guidance are critical to your project success as you get started.

Pareto Selection Method

Pareto charts are your best tools for initially focusing your project in the right direction. Based on the Pareto Principle—that 80% of trouble derives from 20% of the problems—Pareto charts separate factors and chart them in descending order from most troublesome to least. Based on specific financial histories, they help you pick projects by locating waste streams that you can identify and fix or at least reduce. They are powerful, predictive tools that look at performance patterns and prioritize various levels of waste according to the individual project. At a project's inception, the Pareto analysis is actually composed of a three-level charting process.

Here's an example of how it works. Some department at your company is causing waste. Presumably, but not necessarily, the department that costs the most to operate stands the best chance of having waste. So which one is it and what's going on that is causing you to lose dollars?

First, to determine which department is costing your company the most, we chart all the departments, with the Pareto chart for departments (Figure 8-1), using "clean" data (not opinions).

Next, once we've figured out that Department 31 is clearly the most costly to run, then we drill down to the next level of analysis and look at the costs associated with each operation within it, in the Pareto chart for operations (Figure 8-2). This identifies which operation (in this case, OP-40) is costing the most and can be corrected to achieve the most savings.

Now we know which operation is the most costly. We then

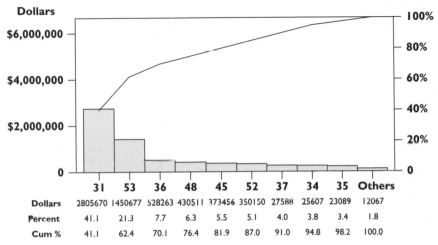

Figure 8-1. Pareto chart for departments (first level)

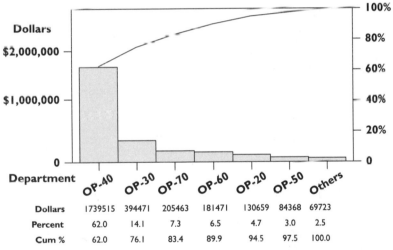

Figure 8-2. Pareto chart for dollars by operations (second level)

look into all of its process steps to figure out which ones are the main sources of the defects and expense. This is where you can also sort out the non-value-added activities and determine which need to go. (You may recall from Chapter 2 that we define value-added as anything critical to a customer that he or she is willing to pay for, such as processing an order, painting a product, etc. Non-value-added activities include material handling, sorting, tool changes, paperwork, etc.)

This is the third part of the analysis, as represented in Pareto chart for OP-40 by Step (Figure 8-3). It's clear that, in this case, the extrusion process leads in costs. Once you know this

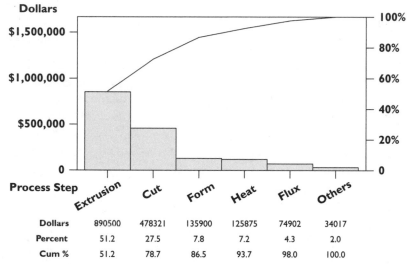

Process Step	Extrusion	Cut	Form	Heat	Flux	Others
Dollars	890500	478321	135900	125875	74902	34017
Percent	51.2	27.5	7.8	7.2	4.3	2.0
Cum %	51.2	78.7	86.5	93.7	98.0	100.0

Figure 8-3. Pareto chart for OP-40 by step (third level)

fact, you can get to the individual issues that are negatively affecting its cost of goods sold.

Now you know the vital few factors and have a good picture of how to focus the project for maximum results. The Pareto selection method is a very handy tool for getting to the heart of the issues in advance of initiating a project. When you conduct the analysis using the drill-down, three-chart method, you arrive at the exact point of defect. You can then implement a project using MAIC to return that lost revenue to your bottom line.

Good vs. Bad Projects

We've discussed the earmarks of "good" Six Sigma projects. Now let's consider the attributes of "bad" projects in a little more detail.

Why? Because they bear an uncanny resemblance to good projects and can really bog down your efforts. These projects rate poorly in terms of one or more of the attributes discussed at the beginning of this chapter—they have little or no business impact, the effort expended is not justified by the results, and the probability of success (that you'll find the money) is not high.

Impact

First, let's look at four aspects that make a poor project with regard to its overall impact on business.

1. *Revising reports.* As interesting as it may be to continually create and revise reports for projects, such activity doesn't get you any money. Again, while further refining such material might make you feel better, there's no tangible, bottom-line outcome. Don't get lost in project materials management; stay focused on the explicit objective.

2. *Quantifying the performance of a process.* This is the "getting ready to get ready" scenario, where you or a black belt spend time stating how good or bad something is without actually fixing it. To put it bluntly, who cares? Again, there's no tangible, positive result that comes of it. Your energies would be much better invested getting to work on the problem.

3. *Improving a supplier's performance without sharing in the benefit.* You depend on a supplier for a key component in your processes and that component is defective. So you help the supplier improve that component. That's good, right? Not necessarily. While it makes sense to have your supplier fix the component so your processes are improved, why would you just give away that corrective measure to the supplier? When you transfer your knowledge, there has to be something in it for you.

4. *Reducing cycle time for an operation that's not critical.* A common pitfall is to focus on reducing cycle time for an operation that's not a bottleneck. Look at it this way: it's not hurting you, but you're fixing it anyway. Again, Six Sigma is

about getting financial results. Your projects must reflect that to succeed.

Effort

Second, a project can be considered to be poor in terms of the effort it requires. Here are some examples:

1. *Installing a company-wide computer network.* This is a huge undertaking with a long time horizon. It does not require a black belt to initiate the MAIC phases to manage it. It's not a problem; it's a business decision. So, for something like this, you just need to "do it"! Deploy your Six Sigma teams elsewhere.
2. *Improving the profitability of an entire product line.* Here the scope of the project is so massive and complex that you probably won't get the results you're looking for in a defined time span. This type of all-encompassing approach is like trying to "boil the ocean"—it's an exercise in frustration when you're trying to get fast, quantifiable results.
3. *Fixing the annual planning process.* Strategic actions such as these are not appropriate for Six Sigma projects. Why? You don't need to assign a black belt to lengthy, administrative tasks; his or her efforts are much better spent on tactical, results-oriented activities.

Probability of Success

Finally, a poor project can be evaluated with regard to its probability of success. A project is unlikely to succeed if any of the following conditions holds:

- If it involves improving a process that won't show any substantial benefits for several months.
- If it depends on the completion of other risky projects.
- If it requires assistance from extremely busy people.
- If it is not aligned with management objectives.

Again, this type of effort lacks definition, schedule, or clear measurement. Without a disciplined, targeted approach and

clearly defined and quantified objectives, projects
may not yield the hidden
dollars you want.

Successful Project Characteristics

Selecting the right project
ultimately comes down to
understanding how it will
fulfill your customer's
expectations of quality,
cost, and delivery while
also driving savings to

> **Be SMART**
>
> A quick and easy way to remember the key aspects of a successful project is found in the acronym, SMART. A project that is SMART is:
> - Specific
> - Measurable
> - Achievable
> - Realistic
> - Time-bound
>
> By keeping these attributes at the forefront of everything you do, your projects will stay on the right track.

your bottom line. To help get you started, I've compiled the following list to itemize key project characteristics you want to see
in any Six Sigma project you undertake. Please remember that
you have to keep the focus on achieving tangible, measurable
results. No matter what the project profile, it must reflect and
return that commitment to you in real, quantifiable dollar terms.
This list can help validate your activities as it addresses some
essential aspects of building successful project outcomes.

Key Project Characteristics

- Your project will increase sales, either by unit volume or
  net price.
- Your project will reduce accounts receivable and net
  inventory or increase accounts payable.
- Your project will reduce actual spending.
- Your project will avoid costs not currently incurred, but
  that would otherwise be very probable.
- Your project will reduce cycle time on critical path steps
  in a bottleneck operation and set the pace for all other
  operations within its supply chain.
- Your project will improve quality and service levels, as
  measured by the customer.

- Project recommendations can be determined and implemented and show results in three months.
- Potential recommendations are unlikely to require a major investment in capital or expense or be thwarted by upper management.
- Historical data on process performance is readily available.
- Your project solution is not already known and will be a true learning experience.
- Your project will focus on a problem that has resisted previous lower-intensity efforts to solve it.
- Your project will help achieve your objectives.
- Your project team members are willing, able, and available to fully support your objectives.
- You have personal knowledge of the process and the project to address it.

There are numerous issues and challenges involved in selecting projects. When you take the top-down approach of Six Sigma and address your strategic objectives and customer expectations, you can get to the operational factors that have the greatest impact. When you select projects that isolate the key processes that are costing you the most—often in almost invisible ways—you can unlock that hidden revenue. If you consider that the average Six Sigma project returns a minimum of $175,000 to the bottom line, the benefits of implementing the disciplined, data-driven methodology speak for themselves. Like anything else worth doing, it takes time and training to learn how to best select Six Sigma projects. Once you've done that, you reap the exponential benefits of each and every project's return on investment.

Manager's Checklist for Chapter 8

❑ Be judicious in your project selection process! Not every business decision is a project and not every project idea will generate the results you want. Choose projects that offer a high-value payoff on a limited amount of effort.

❏ Be sure your projects have a demonstrated cost savings component; after all, you're doing this for the money and you need to be sure you'll find it. Simply, when you locate the cost of poor quality in your process, you locate the savings.

❏ Everyone needs to be on your team—upper management to line workers. Make sure they all understand and support your intensive search for rooting out cost drivers.

❏ Develop good project problem and objective statements. This way, you and your team will always be clear about what you're attacking and why.

❏ Use the drill-down, Pareto three-chart method. The up-front effort is well worth it in terms of unearthing accurate and precise data that shape the course and results of your project.

❏ Remember to include your outside consultant when first selecting projects; tap his or her expertise for maximum value.

❏ Dodge the "bad project" bullet by knowing the warning signs: little or no business impact, poor probability of success, and results that don't justify your efforts.

❏ Keep your project on track by being vigilant about its objectives and how you're going to reach them.

How to Sustain Six Sigma

The best Six Sigma projects begin not inside the business but outside it, focused on answering the question, how can we make the customer more competitive?
—Jack Welch (1935-)

Making your customers more competitive is a key sign that you're successfully implementing Six Sigma. If your performance meets or exceeds the customers' expectations for quality, delivery, and cost, then all your hard work in problem-solving projects has achieved its objective. But is that where it ends?

Of course not. You don't make the investment in Six Sigma and take the time to train people, to select projects, and then to drill down to your costs of poor quality *once*. Six Sigma is ongoing; it's a constant, "living" methodology that needs to continue as long as your business does.

Naturally, individual projects that fix specific problems have start and finish times, but as part of your Six Sigma commitment, you need to initiate new projects, find more dollars, raise your quality levels, and maintain the momentum of your initiative. To get the best return on your investment and keep customers competitive and content, you need to *sustain the gain.*

So how do you do it? How do you avoid the seemingly inevitable outcome of decreasing momentum and declining participation?

Well, the honest answer is that it's not easy. In fact, it's the hardest thing to do—even harder than learning how to use all the statistical tools! However, it's essential. No matter how difficult it may be, you must strive to keep Six Sigma alive. Otherwise, your customers will eventually feel the negative effects of its disappearance and, therefore, so will you.

But there are a few key indicators and guidelines that you can put in place to prevent that from happening and to keep the energy level high. That's the purpose of this chapter.

Basic Infrastructure Requirements

If you look at the basic infrastructure required for successful Six Sigma, it's helpful to break it up into a two-year context. In the first year, you lay a foundation for success. In the second year, you follow up on your successful start and build on that foundation.

In the first year, you need to do the following:

- Set up your database for lessons learned.
- Develop your ongoing project list that registers both projected and actual savings.
- Establish your ongoing communication plan, both externally and internally.
- Grow your black belt and green belt populations.
- Create compensation plans and progression plans for a full two years.
- Develop a common metric and reporting/review system that evaluates and updates the status of all projects monthly.

In the second year, you need to do the following:

- Engage your key suppliers in the Six Sigma methodology.
- Build Six Sigma goals into company-wide strategic plans.
- Host quarterly reviews with senior management.
- Host certification events that reward and recognize black belt achievements.
- Develop compensation/incentive plans that include not just black belts and team members, but also upper management, to ensure continued support.
- Get each black belt to work on four to six projects a year.
- Create a "pull" system for the Six Sigma initiative; publicize the benefits so widely that you turn away potential black belt candidates because your classes are consistently full.
- Determine the next year's goals in the number of black belts, green belts, master black belts, project selection, and savings projections.

As you make progress with Six Sigma, all of these elements will become routine and obvious aspects of the overall scope. However, this is where it's most important to recognize that there's no room for complacency or easing off on Six Sigma projects—sustaining their gains is critical to the continual success of your initiative. All of the items listed point in one direction: keep it focused, keep it moving forward, and keep it in the forefront of everything you do.

Lessons Learned

The first thing you need to do is build and maintain a database of "lessons learned." That means documenting what you've learned and achieved with projects to date and then relying on and sharing that information. Once you've fixed something, you need to be able to share what you know about it. It's important to share the lessons far and wide, not only to tout your success, but also to address similar issues elsewhere in the organization. There's not a lot of value in eliminating defects and keeping it to yourself—knowledge transfer needs to happen continually, both inside and outside of the project at hand.

Communication Plan

A communication plan is essential for sharing lessons learned and sustaining your Six Sigma success. Whether it's press releases, monthly newsletters, company intranet updates, video presentations, or quarterly company meetings, you need to get the message out regularly and conspicuously to people inside and outside the organization.

You can report on the progress of projects, itemize actual dollar savings to date, explain Six Sigma acronyms, or focus in on the key tools. What's essential is to keep getting the word out on the benefits of Six Sigma.

As you know, all levels of personnel should be familiar with the basics of your Six Sigma mission, including terminology, roles, and metrics. This is to ensure that people can "link" between the big picture and actionable items in their different areas. Again, it's all about communicating, in real terms, the powerful implications of each and every project.

Training for Six Sigma

When you start Six Sigma, you focus on training black belts, since they're the tactical leaders of each and every project. What about green belts? Well, when you start out, the ratio of black belts to green belts is about one to three. However, by the time you start the second year, green belts generally increase to about 10% of your company's population.

That increase is based on ever-expanding projects and hands-on expertise, not just by training more candidates for the job. Why? Because the information is being passed throughout the organization. As black belts and green belts become more proficient, they reach out to train others. The exponential benefit is impressive; you must keep the momentum alive by fully recognizing and exploiting this new resource by putting the black belts and green belts to work on new projects.

You can also take this one step further by requiring that all your staff members be trained as green belts; in this way, you are assured that the majority will not only understand, but also participate in the entire Six Sigma initiative. In fact, this training in and of itself can be a project for black belts, as they take on the training responsibility for green belts in their areas.

At least 70% of your black belts should be certified in the first year of your initiative. How are they certified? By completing a minimum of two projects with financial benefits that are independently confirmed by the company controller. (You may remember that in Chapter 4 we discussed the importance of including and informing the controller's department. This becomes even more evident when you seek certification.) Black belts also undergo a tool assessment, an investigation into whether or not they're using the tools correctly. It looks at how they're interpreting the data and whether or not they're getting the maximum financial results from it.

Certification basically translates to a confirmation that your black belts are doing what they're supposed to, that they're following the DMAIC/MAIC method and using the key tools to unearth defects and dollars. Black belts also need to demonstrate a complete list of backlog projects. Simple as it sounds, if you don't have a list of your backlog projects, you're going to have trouble sustaining the gain. Why? Because of the Six Sigma discipline of documenting and quantifying what you're going to work on, why you're going to work on it, and when. It's essential that this be communicated.

On top of this, you need to keep your black belt retention rates high. You want to keep at least 75% of your black belts focused and working on Six Sigma projects. You want to aim for a dropout rate of no more than 5% and have a structured plan to replace dropouts. Given the scope of the investment in every aspect, it's critical that you maintain and grow what you've started. Your success in this area can best be measured by filling black belt training classes. Remember that Six Sigma is an ongoing process: you need to keep spreading the message and methodology throughout the organization to keep retrieving those hidden dollars.

Black Belt Certification Events

Along with certifying black belts goes formally recognizing their accomplishments. As they meet or exceed their individual objectives, you must celebrate their successes, along with the company's overall results.

By hosting certification events, you send a clear signal that black belts and their efforts are highly valued. It's essential to do so—no matter what the individual rank, the project scope, or the dollar value realized, you must demonstrate your appreciation for a job well done. This has ramifications far beyond creating a "feel-good" atmosphere: it shows how seriously you take the Six Sigma work the back belts are doing and what's in it for those who actively participate.

Company Culture

Linking all of your recognition of Six Sigma contributors to the structure of your compensation plans gives you a powerful motivator at the employee level to sustain the gain!

Recognition Pays

Smart Managing

When you publicly acknowledge the successful performance of black belts and their team members, you acknowledge that the investment in Six Sigma has paid off for all parties—company and individuals. Recognition events signal the impact and relevance of Six Sigma projects and indicate just how positive and profitable they are. They *certify* that black belts have mastered the necessary skills required for eliminating defects in any given process.

Depending on your company size and culture, these certification events can take the form of awards dinners, percentage bonuses, or other incentive packages. They can range from lavish and elaborate occasions to more simple incentive programs, depending on your company culture and size. But whatever the form of recognition, when you emphasize the results achieved, the black belt reward structure speaks to others and inspires them to attain black belt status. Certification events are highly motivating public relations tools that really promote each individual success and help net you even more down the road.

Rewarding master black belts, black belts, and green belts for their efforts virtually guarantees sustained interest and energy. You need to establish compensation plans to keep the skill and expertise you've invested so much to develop.

Think about it: how can you avoid a "brain drain," where you lose the entire investment in Six Sigma personnel? Obviously, there's going to be some attrition as people's circumstances change, as they get promoted or they leave the company. You can minimize the losses, however, by clearly communicating and committing to a specifically structured, incentive-based compensation plan for all those involved in Six Sigma at any level.

From executives to line workers, managers to support staff, the compensation plan is a proven tool for keeping the Six Sigma fire burning brightly in the organization. When you "metric" individual performance and tie bonuses to outcomes, you can be assured that your projects will continue to turn in the results you want.

Signs of Success

As you look at the progression of your Six Sigma initiative in its first two years of life, you'll see certain patterns emerging, if you've implemented it correctly. There are certain characteristics to each year's efforts that indicate how well you're sustaining its methodology.

Here's what you want in the first year:

- Train the best of the best for black belt projects.
- Experience dropout rates under 5%.
- Break even within approximately eight months after the initial training.
- Begin the backlog of projects and actively manage the reviews.
- Establish process metrics and set baseline data into strategic plans for the next year.

- Set up the database that captures savings and lessons learned.
- Discover two to four master black belts upon the completion of training.
- Get green belt training under way.

Whether or not you accomplish all of these things is determined by individual company structures and other real-world issues. However, this list of "signs of success" remains the right place to start. Although this may seem repetitive or obvious to you, it's essential that you put in place structures to monitor your progress right from the start. Otherwise, how can you assess what and how well you are doing?

As you move into your second year as a seasoned Six Sigma expert, here are some other signs of success:

- Your internal master black belts are training black belts.
- Dollar savings increase by 300% over the first year's targets.
- Green belts represent 10% of your company population.
- All training has transitioned from an outside consultant to your own company resources.
- Communication is ongoing, externally and internally.
- Black belts are being promoted.
- The project backlog represents no more than 3% to 5% of company revenue.

Again, some of this may look like wishful thinking when set against your particular reality. But consider the benefits of a self-sustaining and exponential Six Sigma initiative when properly and consistently implemented: you and your company are poised to sustain huge gains and expand them as each year passes. Doing so relies on keeping Six Sigma an active, fully focused part of the company's mission and strategy. If you can work toward that goal and remain committed to fostering the application of Six Sigma in all departments, you'll see the enduring results and return on investment you want.

Company Cycles

Make your suppliers a part of your Six Sigma world. You want them involved in your initiative because, depending on your industry, if you're engaged in making or servicing something, chances are good that you use their parts or processes to complete it. Obviously, they affect your defect levels and waste streams.

Basically, you want to train them and get them up to speed with Six Sigma so they can fix or eliminate defects before they reach you. You can leverage both Six Sigma standards and your supplier relationships to further effective, positive, and lasting change in this area. It's in the best interests of your

Agitating for Answers

I recently consulted with a major appliance manufacturer that had a chronic problem with its washing machines: the agitators routinely did not fit. A one-person task of inserting the agitator often became a two-person job of force-fitting the agitator into the washer. Naturally, customers eventually paid the price for this defect: washing machines that didn't work properly. The cost of poor quality soared when field technicians couldn't fix the problem and had to return the machines to the plant. The cost of this problem amounted to $1 million annually.

The black belt assigned to the problem asked why the agitators sometimes fit and sometimes didn't. He examined all aspects of the part and determined that the weights of the agitators were inconsistent.

It turned out that the supplier had never *weighed* the agitators! Getting the supplier involved in the project fixed the problem at its source—before the agitators even arrived at the manufacturing plant! The supplier went back through its processes: it examined its 10 injection molds, identified those that were the source of the weight variation, and then corrected the problem, so that all agitators were weighted correctly and uniformly.

Everybody in the supply chain won and captured the dollars previously lost in returns, restocking, rework, and the high cost of poor quality that affected them all. And, most important, the company was able to consistently meet customers' expectations of quality.

top 10 suppliers to conform to your new standard of quality—not only to retain your business, but also to actually improve their own, simply by embracing the core attributes of Six Sigma.

Partnering with suppliers is an excellent source of improvement and savings; by equally sharing in the techniques, tools, and dollar savings, both parties benefit tremendously. Again, it's a long-term view that yields both short- and long-term results. Look into how and where you can do the same with your primary suppliers, because it's an excellent example of how to pick low-hanging fruit.

Reinforcement and Control

It's also necessary for executive management to regularly review and oversee the entire Six Sigma initiative. This is important to reinforce the depth of the Six Sigma commitment and to keep senior leaders involved and engaged in the process. At least quarterly, senior executives should know and understand the progress of all current projects, the financial results achieved, and the projects ahead.

Six Sigma planning should be built into the business plan; it should be considered an integral element of any strategic planning. As goals are set, Six Sigma personnel and projects should be included as key to achieving them. Six Sigma, over time, must become part of the "genetic code" of the business, an integral part of every tactic and strategy. As noted in Chapter 5, that's an executive responsibility, to make sure that Six Sigma becomes part of the "genetic code" of the company, by inspiring and promoting a Six Sigma culture throughout the organization.

One way to ensure that you're sustaining Six Sigma properly is to use a "sustainability checklist" (Table 9-1). That's a methodical, clear approach to knowing whether or not you're managing to keep the fire burning.

Six Sigma is a pervasive and active methodology. Its benefits are too plentiful to relegate it to a sideline role in the vague hope you might get some benefit from it. It works because it's constant and obvious and because it permeates your company.

Keeping Six Sigma at the forefront keeps your tangible financial gains at the forefront too.

The 21-Question Status Check

The following 21 questions are an excellent guide to assessing the sustained performance of your Six Sigma initiative. By routinely examining and reinforcing your mission with this status check, you minimize the potential for slipping or slacking in company-wide projects. Keep asking and keep answering these fundamentally important questions and you'll keep your initiative on track:

1. Do you think the Six Sigma process is self-sustaining in your group?
2. What is the status of your master black belts?
3. What is the status of your green belts?
4. How many reviews do your senior executives attend?
5. What are the dropout rates?
6. How many projects are officially completed?
7. How many black belts are ready for certification?
8. Has the finance department been an active part of the process?
9. Have you and the finance department agreed on the guidelines that define true savings?
10 Do you currently have a manual system for tracking the backlog list of black belt projects by plant?
11 Do you have the next set of black belts identified and is upper management supportive?
12. Do you think you are focusing on implementing project completions?
13. Are you attempting to change the program or staying with the black belts' focus?
14. Should you stop doing Six Sigma?
15. What is the status report you are giving to senior management?
16. Are the controllers signing off on your projects?
17. Are the controllers aware of the savings?
18. If you were to spot-check the controllers, what defect rate would you find? (In other words, how many do not know about the savings achieved by the projects?)
19. What database are you going to use through the life of tracking your Six Sigma projects?

Table 9-1. Sustainability checklist

20. What is the status of the black belt incentive program discussed at the beginning of the Six Sigma initiative?
21. What are the consequences for champions not helping and driving black belts?

All these questions are highly relevant and thought-provoking. And all your answers must be true and backed up by proof, not assumptions, to keep the momentum going.

The last question is directed at you, specifically, as a manager. You need to honestly examine whether or not you're removing barriers and supporting black belts in their efforts to achieve financial results. If you're not, then you need to take the necessary steps to do so. Remember: black belts and project teams see you as the motivating force, the initiator of the culture change required to identify and remove defects!

Table 9-1. Sustainability checklist., continued

The proof that Six Sigma works is its financial impact on the bottom line—you can't misread the dollar savings! Sustaining Six Sigma takes commitment and leadership; you must be constantly striving to reinforce its value while introducing it further and further down the line to other employees. By making sure that your results are broadcast, that your black belt team is solid, and that your executive staff promotes the methodology, you will be well positioned to *sustain the gain*.

Manager's Checklist for Chapter 9

❏ Managers play a key role in sustaining Six Sigma. By developing a database of lessons learned, you can share your findings and techniques for future applications.

❏ Recognize that you must sustain and expand the initial enthusiasm, commitment, and training and the project results you achieve. If you do it right, your results and the momentum will only build! Determine and communicate your expectations for the first year of Six Sigma and for the second.

❑ You need to establish and maintain a good communication plan to keep everybody current on your Six Sigma initiative. Use company meetings, newsletters, e-mail, or any other appropriate vehicle to keep awareness high.

❑ Support continual training programs for Six Sigma. Training should take place throughout the organization, both formally and informally. Black belts should train green belts and you should increase the number of champions and master black belts: sharing knowledge spreads the Six Sigma message far and wide.

❑ Key to sustaining Six Sigma is to institute a pay-for-performance incentive plan. By linking a bonus structure to project outcomes, you'll maintain the methodology throughout the company.

❑ Host specific black belt certification events. These are vital to demonstrating both the power of the Six Sigma methodology and showing your recognition and rewards for a job well done.

❑ Involve your key suppliers in your Six Sigma initiative. Often, some aspect of their product or service may contain a hidden defect that ultimately costs you with customers. By partnering to root out defects, you and your supplier both win from the improved productivity.

❑ Be sure senior executives visibly support and endorse Six Sigma with regular reviews. As long as upper management signal that they care about and believe in the initiative, its strategic importance is clear to all.

❑ Maintain a Six Sigma sustainability checklist. This is an excellent tool for measuring the health of your initiative over time.

Six Sigma
Proof Positive

*There is one rule for industrialists and that is: Make the
best quality of goods possible at the lowest cost possible,
paying the highest wages possible.*
                    —Henry Ford (1863-1947)

So, now that you've read about the basic how-to's of Six
Sigma, what do you think? Is it possible to deliver the best
quality goods at the lowest cost *and* compensate people fairly?
Once again, the answer is a resounding yes—if you implement
Six Sigma and maintain it over time to get those results.

It's a simple enough formula: give your customers what they
want, when they want it, at a competitive price—their critical-to-
quality (CTQ) factors—and your company can emerge as the
highest-quality, lowest-cost provider. At the same time, retaining
people in whom you've invested time and training is essential,
and that's best accomplished by compensating and rewarding
them with wages and bonuses that truly reflect their high value.
When you do this, you demonstrate your level of commitment

to making it work by sending the clear message that you want results and that you'll do what it takes to get them. It shows your employees that your commitment isn't theoretical. By lobbying for and getting them competitive compensation, in effect you're telling them that you mean business, that you're committing to supporting their satisfaction as they're committing to the customers' satisfaction by deploying Six Sigma full time, front and center.

Where's the downside? There isn't one—everyone's CTQ factors are being met and sustained. As automobile giant Henry Ford said, highest-quality, lowest-cost products delivered by well-paid employees is the single most important business rule of all—and it's a rule that will yield continual results. In all the definitions, phases, project selection, statistical tools, and personnel training issues you've read about here so far, the Six Sigma bottom line is to make sure your bottom line continues to grow—to return hidden revenue to the balance sheet and boost your productivity at every level.

OK, so you know this by now. After all, it's the main theme of this book and the central message of Six Sigma. "Where's the proof?" I can imagine you saying. Well, that's what you're going to see in this chapter.

I'm going to show you the proof, with final reports and real case studies, and give you actual examples of how to recruit, train, and retain quality personnel to serve as black belts and green belts. (There's also a section on champion training and definitions that pertains to you in your managerial capacity.) While this may seem repetitive, it really isn't, because the information in this chapter can serve as your template for launching your own initiative. Further, from the case studies to each job description and on to the next level of Six Sigma, you'll see all of the information you've read about in the preceding chapters come together coherently and effectively. It's proof positive that Six Sigma works.

Real Final Reports

Once you've defined your project, the team's been trained, the metrics are in place, the team has used the MAIC method, and the results are in—then what? Well, that's when you and your black belts sit down and compile all you've learned into a final report.

That final report is more than a mere summary of your project activities or an accounting of expenses incurred. It's a comprehensive statement of work and an excellent reference tool for future projects. It thoroughly examines each project objective and the steps taken. It delivers an overview that plots the process and indicates where the defects were found, what statistical tools were used to identify them, how the black belt determined corrective action, and the resulting savings.

To be effective, final reports need to include certain key elements that present and quantify a given project's objectives. While each one is unique to the problem addressed, there are seven basic sections that you need to incorporate in each report. Within each, you can get as specific as necessary about a given project in terms of how you went about measuring, analyzing, improving, and controlling the problem. These are the seven main sections to develop:

Final Report Facts

Each final report becomes a milestone on your Six Sigma roadmap. They are invaluable resources for indicating the sequential nature of projects and why it's necessary to proceed that way. Remember that you don't want opinions; you want data. Final reports present you with the facts to fix the defects in a disciplined, logical sequence.

Smart Managing

1. Executive Summary
   1.1 Main Problem
   1.2 Project Goals
   1.3 Project Results

2. Problem Statement
   2.1 Customer Requirements
   2.2 Project Objectives
   2.3 Outline of Project Strategy
   2.4 Project Schedule
   2.5 Final Project Description
3. Experimental Data (actions taken)
   3.1 Gauge Studies
   3.2 Materials Characterization (if appropriate)
   3.3 Process Specifications
   3.4 Capability Studies (short and long term)
   3.5 Design of Experiments
4. Implementation
   4.1 Operating Specification
   4.2 Process FMEA
   4.3 Performance Tracking Systems
   4.4 Performance Data
   4.5 Support Systems
   4.6 Control Plans
5. Conclusions
   5.1 Discussion of Results
   5.2 Lessons Learned/Recommendations
6. Team Member Listing
7. Data Storage

Since all projects are not created equal, each final report must address the unique concerns and conclusions of each one within these main sections and their subsections. (This is where you get to demonstrate your use of the statistical tools you learned about in Chapter 7.) The main headings are a place to start understanding the basics of a final report. As you conduct each project, you can include the critical information that you and the project team have gathered to justify the project's goals and demonstrate how and why you reached your conclusions.

Case Studies

To understand better how the theoretical is transformed into real-world application, how you can deploy Six Sigma to drive down defects and drive up profitability, it helps to examine actual cases of Six Sigma projects. Even though this book has presented and discussed the method, tools, personnel, and other project management aspects, it's valuable to take a look at individual projects across the spectrum of industry, to get a sense of the method in action. Once you take a good look at these case studies, you'll also see how their progression and functions are absolutely mirrored by the sequence and detail of the final reports just discussed. These case studies put into perspective just how valuable a final report is, both to illustrate the project just concluded and to serve as a case study for future project teams.

Case Study #1: Fulfilling Government Orders

A company that counts a large government agency as one of its customers repeatedly experienced some significant cash flow and receivables problems associated with this account. The company (we'll call it Company X) needed to free up this bottleneck to improve cash flow and better manage receivables.

The Main Issue. A government customer issued a significant number of unpriced orders for specialized products. Because of Company X's long administrative time frames, it often shipped these products to the customer before the company and the agency agreed on prices for the products. This practice led to Company X experiencing a constant level of $13 million in nominal receivables for these orders, which reduced its cash flow and directly cost up to $400,000 in tied-up capital.

The Project. The goal of this project was to reduce by 85% the total receivables trapped due to unpriced orders.

The Strategy. The black belt and his project team went to work using the MAIC method and deploying statistical tools within each of its phases to figure out where and how the bottlenecks were occurring. They mapped the existing process and then developed an alternative one to correct the variations within it.

"M" is for Measure. The team introduced measurements into the order issue, entry, scheduling, proposal, and negotiation phases of the process, using the existing MIS system to flag out-of-control phases against certain time specifications.

"A" is for Analyze. The team set targets for order processing times for each phase of the order process. Charts were used to monitor performance at each stage and out-of-control exceptions were noted and investigated.

"I" is for Improve. Once the measurements and analysis were complete, the black belt had the data he needed to approach the customer to resolve the consequence of unpriced orders. Those negotiations resulted in Company X being able to bill 75% of the proposed value of the order at the time of shipment. A tracking report for unpriced orders was introduced, with a policy change to first in, first out (FIFO) order processing.

"C" is for Control. Permanent changes were introduced into Company X's MIS system for handling and monitoring unpriced orders. As a result of this project, further work is anticipated in the overall order entry process. Additionally, the customer and the company are both working to reduce the use of the unpriced order process.

The Results. The black belt and his team reduced the amount of receivables trapped by unpriced orders by 96%, which was well in excess of their original 85% target. This resulted in $12.5 million being freed up during the four months of the project's duration. The company saved $300,000 to $400,000 per year in financing charges.

Case Study #2: Scrapping Defects in Manufacturing

Managers at a manufacturing company that we'll call Company Y were generally aware that certain defects in a component were resulting in a lot of scrap, which caused a money drain.

The Main Issue. On this high-speed rotating component, an oil drain slot, by its location and size, determined the service life of the component, due to the stresses induced. Since the slot was inadequately manufactured, the annual known costs of scrap for it amounted to $170,000.

The Project Goal. The black belt assigned to this situation recognized that the primary goal was to identify and eliminate the inconsistent manufacturing processes that were causing all the scrap and rework. Once she had done that, she could then drive the dollar savings out of these waste streams and into the bottom line. At a minimum, her goal was to save the identified $170,000.

"M" is for Measure. The black belt and her team conducted a gauge R&R (repeatability and reproducibility) study that showed the existing measuring system variation contributed to 17.5% of the total variation being measured on the smallest dimension. Although that was greater than the preferred 10%, it was still less than the recommended maximum of 30%. Measurements of the oil slot dimensions indicated a short sigma value ranging from 0.6 (forward slot axial position) to 65.8 (aft slot parallelism). The black belt and her team started working to identify reasons for the low sigma values.

"A" is for Analyze. A tooling pin that established the alignment of the component in the machining fixture was identified as having a significant run-out (taper) that allowed an out-of-specification location of the component in the fixture. Additionally, the pin holder was identified as being damaged. It was replaced immediately and the axial location sigma values rose to 4.3 from 0.6. By using hypothesis testing, the team identified that tool deflection and tool wear were major causes of deviation from the requirements.

"I" is for Improve. The black belt suggested that a stiffer tool holder be introduced, together with a scheduled program of regular mill tool changes. She then proposed enlarging and changing the slot profile so that a larger milling tool could be introduced and deflect less during use. Following that, the team conducted a simulation study on the impact of the life cycle of the component with the enlarged slot.

"C" is for Control. A trial slot design was then analyzed, together with a complete three-dimensional stress analysis to determine the impact of the change. Changes were made to setups and manufacturing and a further risk analysis was undertaken on the introduction of the new slot design.

The Results. Ultimately, the final throughput yield increased from 28% to 94% for the finished component with the existing slot design, which amounted to nearly double the projected savings, or $309,000 annually.

Case Study #3: Accounting for Delinquent Accounts

Welcome to Company Z, where delinquent customer accounts more than 30 days overdue are costing the company at least $7 million per month!

The Main Issue. Approximately 65% of these overdue accounts result from commercial issues or administrative problems. At current commercial interest rates, this represents a $325,000 annual expense to Company Z, which it can ill afford.

The Project Strategy. The black belt and his team had their work cut out for them on this project. They needed to identify why, where, and how these accounts were becoming overdue and how to change processes to avoid the staggering cost of errors in this transactional environment.

"M" is for Measure. The black belt started by developing primary and secondary metrics to track the progress of this project. First, he categorized monthly delinquent accounts receivable dollars that were less than 30 days overdue, with a baseline of $7 million per month. Then, he segmented the monthly delinquent accounts receivable dollars by total month-end accounts using a baseline of 15% defective. Process maps and interviews were conducted with all personnel throughout each functional area. A new measuring system was installed to assign category and causes to receivable disputes, together with a two-level Pareto analysis of the previous 12 months' disputes. Four issues were identified as contributing to 80% of the commercial disputes, which in turn contributed to 65% of all delinquent accounts.

"A" is for Analyze. The team obtained additional order data, by salesperson, district, region, order type, etc. Hypothesis tests showed *no* significant difference among the groups. But a cause-and-effect matrix and an FMEA isolated a list of five key factors (X's) that were found to be driving the four issues contributing to the commercial disputes. All of these five factors (X's) resulted in sales order information being inconsistent with purchase order/contract information.

"I" is for Improve. The black belt team conducted a designed experiment at the order point to validate these five key factors. As a result, a new corporate policy, MIS procedures, and a training program were initiated.

"C" is for Control. To ensure that the gains were sustained, the black belt instituted a time series analysis and other monitoring devices that would flag any new deviations or backsliding into old process patterns.

The Results. Company Z stopped the financial drain on its resources and greatly improved its cash flow. It saved $325,000 annually and had reliable mechanisms in place that ensured that over time it wouldn't end up where it was before Six Sigma.

Essential Elements of Six Sigma Success

These case studies have one thing in common—dedicated, well-trained black belt teams and support structures that rewarded and championed their efforts in every way possible to get the results they needed. This is another instance that takes us back to an essential ingredient of Six Sigma success—fully trained, fully supported black belts who are free to use what they know to locate and eliminate defects. Your projects—from selection to final reports—all depend on the people you assign to work on them and the ways in which you reward them. Choose your people well and reward them generously; you'll be astounded at the energy, enthusiasm, and end results you generate.

Training Agendas

So now we get into some training and job description issues for your project teams. At this point, you may well be thinking, "Haven't we already gone over this before?" Well, yes, in point of fact, we have. But this is a message that not only bears repeating, but also deserves further definition to give you the most comprehensive understanding of what is involved in training Six Sigma operatives—not just black belts and green belts, but also you in your role as champion.

    An educated and informed champion is in an excellent position to select and direct key staff members as black

---

Championing Your Role

Smart Managing   You already know what the champion does in his or her role in Six Sigma, but you might not be aware of basic training elements that determine how well equipped a person is for the task. You're far more than a cheerleader or magician who makes barriers disappear. A champion must understand what his or her black belts are working with in order to best facilitate their progress. At a minimum, a champion must be trained in the following:
- Project selection methods
- Basic statistics
- Capability analysis
- Measurement systems analysis
- Process mapping
- XY matrix
- Hypothesis testing
- Design of Experiments

    If you know what your black belts are doing, you can better understand all their findings in their final reports and, in turn, present and explain those results to upper management. It's essential that you be well versed in all the tools and methodologies of Six Sigma, in order to be a smart and effective champion.

No Short Cuts to Black Belt Training

CAUTION!

There are no short cuts to black belt training. Both you and your candidates need to know and accept this going in. Each session is extensive, interactive, and consuming. You cannot skip any aspect of it and think you've got what it takes to implement Six Sigma. Like everything else in the methodology, training is sequential and builds on necessary steps. You can't hurry the process. But then, with that Six Sigma training, black belts armed will rapidly transform the organization wherever they apply their skills and knowledge ... and then the pace is lightning fast!

---

belts. Black belt training is extensive, if not exhaustive. You need to be prepared to facilitate and encourage that process to graduate a black belt who has the expertise to deliver on the investment made in his or her training.

It's important to reiterate once again that a black belt is not a part-time role. The time and investment it takes to fully train and equip black belts would never see a return if they did not go to work at Six Sigma full time. Black belts are the catalysts driving the change—they need to have all the information and tools at their disposal in order to make decisions, plot projects, and dig out variation wherever it exists.

Training for black belts basically follows the MAIC sequence. They learn about measuring, analyzing, improving, and controlling processes in intensive, hands-on training sessions that take eight hours a day, five days a week, for a month—30 days of non-stop immersion in learning what makes Six Sigma tick.

Here's a look at what black belt training agendas entail:

Session One: Measure (Week One). Black belts are introduced to Six Sigma; assigned projects; taught process mapping, FMEA matrices, statistics, capability studies, measurement systems and project application; and given regular homework.

Session Two: Analyze (Week Two). Black belts learn how to analyze distributions, graphically plot data, conduct multivariate analyses, do hypothesis testing, and plan project applications while completing regular homework assignments.

Session Three: Improve (Week Three). By week three, black belts are ready to learn the Design of Experiments method, understand correlation studies, conduct full factorial experiments, and continue to plan and execute project plans.

Session Four: Control (Week Four). Digging into all the control tools, black belts now enter the final phase of training by reviewing the methodology, learning how to implement statistical methods of control and mistake proofing, and finalizing their project work.

This is where it all comes together—black belts have the tools, know how to use them, and are ready for you to champion their cause as they take on projects.

In addition, the green belts also receive training in the methodology, so they can assist and support the black belts. Without a working knowledge of the methodology, they would be severely limited in the kinds of assistance and support they could provide. Their training is not as rigorous or detailed as that of the black belts, but green belts receive the necessary guidance to increase their technical knowledge to the point that they become local experts at solving problems—which creates another path to bottom-line savings.

Job Descriptions

As stated earlier, being a champion or a black belt is not a part-time job. All the training and discipline just considered would be a waste of time and money if the champions and black belts didn't put it to use right away full time. These are full-time jobs and, as such, must be treated that way in every respect by companies. To that end, you need job descriptions to define the positions of champion and black belt, in order to elicit interest from potential candidates.

Like any other job description common in business today, these descriptions need to indicate the title, level, reporting structure, purpose, responsibilities, and qualifications required. By developing a standardized job description, you further indicate the permanent, full-time character of Six Sigma.

The following examples of Six Sigma job postings should give you a good idea of what to include.

OPEN POSITION SPECIFICATION POSTING NOTICE

Position Title: Champion
Organization Level:
Business Unit or Organization:
Location of Job:
Position Reports to (Immediate Supervisor): VP level or higher
Position Purpose: The customers that form the enormous base of today's world market are sending a clear and undeniable message—produce higher-quality products at lower cost with greater responsiveness. Numerous companies have heard this message and are visibly rising to the Six Sigma challenge. For many, Six Sigma has led to the breakthrough improvement of business, engineering, manufacturing, service, and administrative processes. Of course, such a process-oriented focus leads to significant reduction in cost and cycle time; however, the principal focus is always on the continuous improvement of customer satisfaction. To this end, the Six Sigma champion certification program was conceived, designed, and developed. The intent of this program is to provide key individuals with the managerial and technical knowledge necessary to facilitate the leadership, implementation, and deployment of Six Sigma. The instructional goal is to transfer and reinforce fundamental Six Sigma strategies, tactics, and tools necessary for achieving breakthroughs in key product designs, manufacturing processes, services, and administrative processes. To best support this focus, the program delivery has been structured into two self-contained segments that, when successfully completed, lead to certification. Naturally, the resulting certificate denotes and communicates a high level of executive commitment, dedication, competency, and leadership.
Qualifications (skills or talents) that a candidate <u>MUST</u> possess to gain consideration for this position:
Must have demonstrated success of leading a team and key individuals to a business result. Demonstrated project management skills. Technical competence in basic statistical calculations and graphical analysis such as Pareto, time series, and correlation. The basic concepts of problem-solving and coaching employees. Proven track record in removing barriers and dealing directly with organizational issues to resolve conflict between and within functional groups. A leader that demonstrates

through actions and follow-up. Competent in basic budget and accounting principles within business units and between functional boundaries.

Additional qualifications that are *desired* in a candidate and will be important in making the final candidate selection: Managerial and technical knowledge necessary to facilitate the leadership, implementation, and deployment of Six Sigma. Ability to understand basic concepts and fit them into realistic implementation action plans. Clearly understands and practices business planning that links to company strategies. Ability to mentor and inspire key individuals and teams to reach new levels of improvement. Ability to negotiate within and between functional groups. A relentless desire to improve the current state of the business. A respected leader inside the company. Ideally suited for the person who is given the task of implementing new projects or initiatives in the company with a proven track record for results.

OPEN POSITION SPECIFICATION POSTING NOTICE

Position Title: Black Belt
Organization Level:
Business Unit or Organization:
Location of Job:
Position Reports to (Immediate Supervisor): Champion and Project Leadership
Position Purpose: Black belts are contributors from various disciplines who, when trained, become change agents for operational excellence. Black belts carry a very high level of peer respect and are clearly seen as leaders—they manage risks, set direction, and lead the way to breakthrough improvement. They are paradigm shifters to help others discover a better improvement process. They should be encouraged to stimulate management thinking by posing new ways of doing things, to challenge conventional wisdom by demonstrating successful application of new methodologies, to seek out and pilot new tools, to create innovative thinking, and to serve as role models for others to follow in their footsteps.

Qualifications (skills or talents) that a candidate <u>MUST</u> possess to gain consideration for this position:
Possess process/product knowledge, basic statistical knowledge, organizational knowledge, and communication skills. Perform work of analytical, detailed, and logical nature. Project management skills are required. Basic

computer skills using Microsoft ® software necessary. Have a detailed understanding of customer requirements and understand basic business practices.

Additional qualifications that are *desired* in a candidate and will be important in making the final candidate selection:

Be a self-starter, open-minded, willing to learn new ideas, desire to drive change and improve current standard, team player, and respected by peers. Basic statistical knowledge. Advance quality planning, FMEA training, statistical process control training. Actively advocate on behalf of project teams. Demonstrate high energy and trustworthiness and be goal oriented.

Job descriptions are a good way to ensure that your candidates are actually up to the responsibilities; by specifying the qualifications necessary, you eliminate unqualified candidates or those with only a superficial interest. This is even more important when you consider the time and resources it takes to train black belts: you want to be as sure as possible that you will be investing in someone with the credentials and motivation to succeed in the long term.

Design for Six Sigma

Looking into the future, the goal is to get the maximum return on your Six Sigma investment by spreading it throughout your company, continuing to grow the black belt population, and sustaining the exponential gains you achieve by keeping it going.

But in addition to the expanding practice of the methodology and dollars redirected to the bottom line, there's another dimension available to consider. Six Sigma doesn't exist in a vacuum; while its principles remain constant, there's an evolution of its message that can

Design for Six Sigma (DFSS) A systematic methodology using tools, training, and measurements to enable the design of products, services, and processes that meet customer expectations at Six Sigma quality levels. DFSS optimizes your design process to achieve Six Sigma performance and integrates Six Sigma characteristics at the outset of new product development with a disciplined set of tools.

Key Term

take companies in exciting new directions. I'm referring to the discipline known as Design for Six Sigma (DFSS).

Robert G. Cooper states in *Winning at New Products: Accelerating the Process from Idea to Launch* (Perseus Books, 2001, 3rd edition) that only about 60% of new products launched are actually a success and that for every seven new product ideas, only four make it to development, and then only one succeeds. What's wrong with this picture? The new product cycle is definitely not operating at a six sigma level. In fact, it's closer to the average four sigma quality level at which many companies operate today. Plus, even as manufacturing problems are corrected by deploying Six Sigma methods, newly developed products often are the source of new problems. So, an organization practicing the methodology in various functional areas and attaining Six Sigma status may well be far below that in developing new products or services.

Once you've mastered the essentials of Six Sigma, you may well be ready for the essentials of DFSS, to carry that improvement into the development and design of your new products. DFSS is based on the notion that when you design Six Sigma quality right at the outset of new product development, it's probable that you'll sustain that gain too as customers accept that item. By incorporating DFSS, you're virtually assured that the product or service you're launching will perform dependably in the marketplace, thus setting it up for very positive acceptance. Like its parent Six Sigma initiative, DFSS uses a disciplined set of tools to bring high quality to launches.

It begins by conducting a gap analysis of your entire product development system. A gap analysis, as explained in Chapter 3, figures out where the gaps are in your processes that are negatively affecting new product performance. It also addresses a highly significant factor, the voice of the customer (VOC). Every new product decision must be driven by the VOC; otherwise, what basis do you have for introducing it? By learning how to identify that voice and responding to it, you're in a far better position to deliver a new product or service that customers actually want!

Once the gap analysis is done and the VOC is identified, DFSS goes to work with its own version of MAIC, but in this case, it's a five-step process:

- **Plan:** enables the team to succeed with the project by mapping all vital steps
- **Identify:** hears the voice of the customer to select the best product concept
- **Design:** builds a thorough knowledge base about the product and its processes
- **Optimize:** achieves balance of quality, cost, and time to market
- **Validate:** demonstrates with data that the voice of the customer has been heard and satisfied

(Some Six Sigma people equate DFSS with another five-step process—DMADV: define, measure, analyze, design, and verify. Others use only the IDOV steps listed above. Design for Six Sigma is relatively new, so we can naturally expect some inconsistencies and evolution of the models as companies and consultants apply them.)

Once again, the success of this Six Sigma offshoot requires the active participation of management. You and upper management must monitor its progress regularly to keep it on course. DFSS can be a very useful tool to companies as they get comfortable with Six Sigma and look to grow its benefits in other areas.

Ultimately, DFSS is not that different from the Six Sigma work you're undertaking. In fact, it's a natural progression to continually—and relentlessly—root out defects and route hidden dollars to the bottom line.

The End ... and the Beginning

In conclusion, let me say that I recognize that for you to grasp all the concepts presented in this book is like trying to drink from the proverbial fire hose. There's a lot to learn about Six Sigma, more than I could cover in these pages. It's not an easy task to under-

take and it's a continually evolving lesson in quality improvement. But, to return to a theme that has permeated this book, in
order for you to fully "get" Six Sigma, you have to dive in and
start practicing it. Although I've broken it down and attempted to
illustrate it as simply as possible, these pages are just theory to
you. When you take the plunge and put it into action, the light will
come on and then you'll be able to say, "Now I get it!"

If you get anything at all from this book, I hope it's these two
things:

- The Six Sigma journey is a full-time trip and never, ever
  ends, as long as you want to attain the pinnacle of quality and grow the bottom line in your role as the highest-
  quality, lowest-cost producer of goods and services.
- To sustain the Six Sigma gain and create a Six Sigma culture, middle managers *must* be relentless in the pursuit of
  this journey by setting it as a priority inside their business
  plans.

After all, as Henry Ford said all those years ago, it's the one
rule by which to conduct a successful business. It's simple. It's
Six Sigma.

Manager's Checklist for Chapter 10

❑ Managers need to be sure that comprehensive final reports
are assembled for each completed project. By doing so,
you create a record of the procedures and processes
involved in a specific project that can serve as a template
for future projects.

❑ It's helpful to consider real-world case studies of Six Sigma
projects. When you recognize just how flexible and valuable the methodology is across various functions, you
appreciate how you can adapt it to your needs.

❑ How you go about training yourself and your teams in Six
Sigma is critically important. It's essential that you as a
champion understand the tools and techniques black belts

use. It's equally important that black belts fully understand these tools to do their jobs.

❏ Knowing the professional responsibilities of both champions and black belts further defines these key roles and credentials. Specific, sequential, and thorough training programs are necessary to gain that knowledge.

❏ Once you have your Six Sigma initiative well under way with existing processes, the next logical step is to examine your new product and/or service development functions. An extension of the methodology, Design for Six Sigma, helps you further improve and control product launches by designing Six Sigma quality right into your development processes.

Index

A
Air Academy, and Six Sigma, 8
AlliedSignal
    savings with Six Sigma, 32
    use of Six Sigma, 7
American Express, use of Six
    Sigma, 7
American Productivity & Quality
    Center, and benchmarking, 58
Analyze phase, 98-99
Assumptions, need to test, 45
Average, *see* Mean

B
Baselines
    defined, 57
    and metrics, 56-57
Belts, *see* Black belts, Green
    belts, Master Black belts
Benchmarking
    American Productivity &
        Quality Center, 58
    defined, 27
    ethics, 58
    International Benchmarking
        Clearinghouse, 58
    legalities, 58
    and metrics, 57-59
Benchmarks
    choosing, 27, 58
    and value, 26-29

Bin
    explained, 109-110
    width, explained, 110
Black belts
    candidates
        rating, 88
        selecting, 75, 87-89
    celebrating, 151
    certification, 150-151
    defined, 12
    job descriptions, 170-173
    master, *see* Master black belt
    responsibilities, 86-87
    role, in brief, 12-13, 80
    training, 75-76, 149-150, 169-
        170
    traits, for success, 88-89
Brainstorming
    defined, 71
    explained, 117
    and XY matrix, 117-120
Breakthrough goals
    and company objectives, 18
    defined, 13
Bucket, *see* Bin
Business metrics, *see* Metrics

C
Capability, process
    analysis, 121-123
    defined, 9

179